Aunts

A Celebration

of Those

Special Women

in Our Lives

Annette Sara Cunningham

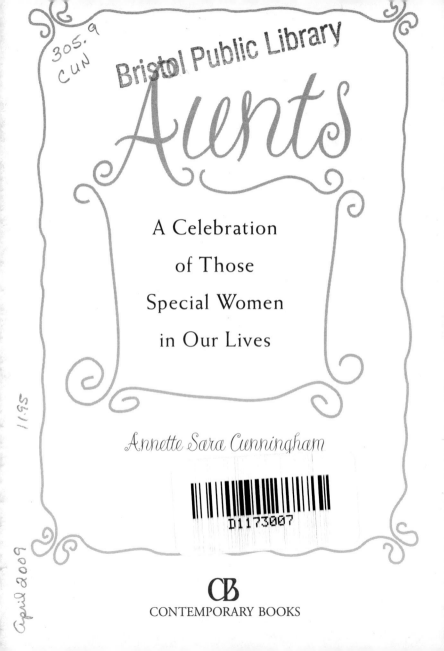

D1173007

CB
CONTEMPORARY BOOKS

Library of Congress Cataloging-in-Publication Data

Cunningham, Annette Sara.
    Aunts: a celebration of those special women in our lives /
Annette Sara Cunningham.
        p.   cm.
      ISBN 0-8092-3057-7
      1. Aunts.   I. Title.
    HQ759.94.C85   1997
    305.9'046—dc21   97-20728
                                                    CIP

Cover design by Monica Baziuk
Interior design by Mary Lockwood

Published by Contemporary Books
An imprint of NTC/Contemporary Publishing Company
4255 West Touhy Avenue, Lincolnwood (Chicago), Illinois
60646-1975 U.S.A.
Copyright © 1998 by Annette Sara Cunningham
All rights reserved. No part of this book may be reproduced,
stored in a retrieval system, or transmitted in any form or by any
means, electronic, mechanical, photocopying, recording, or
otherwise, without the prior permission of NTC/Contemporary
Publishing Company.
Printed in the United States of America
International Standard Book Number: 0-8092-3057-7

15   14   13   12   11   10   9   8   7

*T*his book is dedicated to the people who gave me the credentials to write it—relatives at first, friends later, and always beloved: John Cunningham Luby, James Russell Fay Jr., Patrick Michael Fay, Meagen Fay-Gunther (who is responsible for much of what is funny in this book, and a great deal more as well), Sara Cunningham Luby-Baluha, Alice Cunningham Luby-Bedell, Edward Charles Fay Sr., Christopher Robert Fay, Kevin Cassin Luby, Meghan Elizabeth Luby, James Russell Fay III, Victoria Mary Luby, John Leo Bedell, Maureen Keely Bedell, Edward Patterson Fay, Audrey Claire Baluha, William Charles Cunningham "Liam" Fay, Thomas Joseph Bedell, McKenna Doherty Fay, Edward Charles Fay Jr., Alex Cunningham Baluha, Colleen Doherty Bedell, Mairead Ann Deirdre "Maudie" Fay, Fiona Isabel Fay Villamar, Warren Clohisy Fay, and Niall Patrick Micael Fay. And to a happy half-dozen of honoraries (including a godchild and namesake) to whom I have always been "Aunt Annette" and whom I hold really dear: Elizabeth Annette Fogerty, William George Cosmas Jr., Robert Lawrence Thomas Fogerty, Maureen Dunphy, Anthony and Ryan Joseph Colella.

Contents

Aunting: *n*, the condition of being related to the child of one's siblings; the honor of being chosen to relate to the child of one's friend; part., the state of continuing activity caused or occasioned by the relationship to children of one's siblings or friends

Overture

*J*f Shakespeare was right and "all the world's a stage," then life is a play (or for that matter, a movie or an opera or a ballet—though it sometimes feels more like a circus), and *the Aunt* is the hands-down winner for that play's "best actress in a supporting role." It may not be the lead, but it has all the makings of a plum part. For one thing, there are lots of opportunities to get cast. Nearly every family has one; most have several; the ones that don't have them by blood get to choose them for other reasons. So, if one Aunt has already been cast, no need to give up. Unlike Mothers and Fathers, there can be an indefinite number of Aunts.

The Aunt's lines can be good, and you even get a chance to improvise and write your own script. The costuming opportunities have improved a lot since the nineteenth century, even since the 1950s.

Aunts are rich, poor, beloved, intimidating, close, distant, young, old, urban, suburban, rural, hip, hidebound, holistic, conservative, banner-carrying, bun-wearing, chic, comfy, born, or inherited. Graham Greene and Patrick Dennis made theirs famous. Dorothy from *The Wizard of Oz* did, too; Rodgers and Hammerstein gave their heroine's Aunt a featured role in *Oklahoma!* It's hard to forget *Anne of Green Gables'* Aunt-figure Marilla or *Tom Sawyer's* Aunt Polly. It's easy to remember "The Andy Griffith Show's" Aunt Bee.

Shirley MacLaine, Wendy Wasserstein, and Liza Minnelli probably come closer to exemplifying the current turn-of-the-century Aunt. In the 1990s, with people marrying later and many having fewer children or none at all, there has emerged a new breed of Aunt for whom the nurturing role is seriously and unselfconsciously important.

If there's a problem with playing the part of *the Aunt*, it's that there are very few stage directions. The role doesn't come with a lot of notes about how the part is supposed to be played. So, when you get down to the specifics, you're pretty much on your own, and that can be both good news and bad.

This book is designed to fill in for the lack of stage directions that could help *the Aunt* play her part. It is a combination handbook for women who get to play *the Aunt*, and "Cliff's Notes" for the people who watch the performance or play other roles in the cast. It is designed to strike a chord with a wide variety of people who will find in these pages reasons to laugh, to remember, to resolve, and to recognize a moment they themselves have experienced or observed but never put into words.

So, if you are, or if you have, or if you know an Aunt, you have a reason to continue reading this book. You'll find in its pages a look at some of the things that go into play-ing the role of *the Aunt* or of understanding someone else's performance. In other words, it's about how to:

get the role, or
understand the role, or
play the role, or
rehearse with the rest of the cast, or
suggest how the role should be played, or
simply, appreciate the role.

I've seen the role of *the Aunt* played by some of the "greats"—the Sarah Bernhardts, Helen Hayeses, and Meryl Streeps of Aunting, so to speak, and it didn't make me too intimidated to try it for myself. That's because the really great ones make playing *the Aunt* look as natural as breath-ing. At this writing, I've been cast in the role twenty-five times (and counting) by blood and countless times by "honor." And I can vouch for the fact that no two perfor-mances are ever the same. So, if you are an Aunt, I hope you will find some common ground between the covers of this book. Plato would, I feel sure, forgive me for para-phrasing his great line to suggest that unexamined Aunt-hood is not worth living. Aunts, you are invited to take this opportunity to examine it, and you may find you have a new regard for what you've been doing all along. Those of you who have an Aunt or know one, I hope you may find happy or funny reminders of her and her role in your life. At the very least you may find yourself saying, "Oh, that's why she always . . ."

I hope that by reading, as either audience or actor, you get to know more about what goes into the role of *the Aunt*. I hope, too, that knowing more about that one role will lead you to a better understanding of the play as a whole and open the way to enjoying it more than ever.

There are just three simple things to remember when looking at *the Aunt* as one of life's really great supporting roles.

First, think of the play as a comedy.

Second, remember that this is not a one-woman show, and success depends on being a good ensemble performer.

Third, get ready to attend the awards ceremonies.

In that spirit, this book is offered as a celebration of Aunts: the ones we are; the ones we have; the ones we know. So, as you read it, prepare to laugh a little, say, "Of course, of course!" a few times, and look at the world of *the Aunt* from a new perspective.

In short, this book is for you: to read or to give to your favorite Aunt. And if you find that some unexpected people give it to you, don't be surprised to discover that they are trying to tell you that you're about to be cast in the supporting role of a lifetime!

Getting the Part

Some are born for the role of the Aunt. They get the part because of family connections when their Sisters or Brothers present them with their first Niece or Nephew. To some Aunts, that happens early, even before they can vote. But there are pluses (and minuses) for the Aunt and her Nieces/Nephews whenever that casting call happens to occur.

Others are "discovered" for the role even though they have no family connections.

For both sets of candidates, though, getting the part and getting to be the real thing are two different matters. Getting the part is always an honor. Getting to be "real" is an achievement.

And I Couldn't Even Vote

I learned about labor and Aunting the same week. At least, I started to. And what I learned was that they are both much bigger deals than I had thought.

As the youngest of four siblings (in the position variously described as afterthought, caboose, or "change-of-life baby") I had not observed pregnancy firsthand. What I knew about the birthing process I owed to G-rated movies when a pristine, starched, and becapped nurse came out to the waiting room to show off an equally pristine baby . . . presumably about ten minutes after the heroine cheerily announced, "It's time, Honey."

When I became an Aunt, reality started to set in. I knew labor had to be something serious, since it kept my Sister Mary from calling me to say "Happy Birthday." (A disappointment for most people; a tragedy for a practicing adolescent.) The "something serious," as it turned out, was two days of labor and my Nephew, John Cunningham Luby, born the day after my birthday. He was singlehandedly responsible for getting me into the Aunting business at an age when the rest of my friends were excited about being in high school, looking forward to their first dates, and feeling—strongly—that it was not cool even to have younger siblings, much less a Niece or Nephew. So, there I was, unable to vote, drink, or drive and already someone's Aunt. For lots of years, John's arrival, and that of James Russell Fay Jr. a year later, shaped my Aunt's-eye view of the world. Long afterward, when each had gone from being Nephew to being my good friend, they became the Fathers of my first two Grand-Nephews (or is it Great?). For that second wave of Nieces and Nephews, I was much more prepared for the role: I had studied; practiced; performed.

There are, of course, distinct benefits to having an "underage Aunt." But there are just as many for having an Aunt who is more the age of a Parent. It's worth doing a sort of quick audit of the relative merits of "underage" Aunts and "mature ones," as seen both from the Aunts' points of view and those of their Nieces and Nephews.

Being an "Underage" Aunt—the Aunt's View

- Now even if my Parents do let me go, no one will ask me to dance. Can't you just imagine . . . "How about a dance, Aunt Annette?" In your dreams!
- It's sort of like having a Cousin. But . . . you're allowed not to like a Cousin. I don't think you're allowed not to like a Niece or Nephew.
- It's bound to make my teachers take me more seriously.

- This must be what it's like to have a little Brother or Sister.

Having an "Underage Aunt"— the Niece/Nephew's View

- I hear older ones give better presents. But, at least I can count on the fact that she doesn't think Pearl Jam is jewelry polish.
- When she comes to pick me up from school, there's some chance people won't connect her with my Mother!
- "Who's the weirdo in my christening pictures wearing a freshman beanie?"
- "I hope that jerk on the senior varsity team thinks she's my girlfriend."
- "I'd just as soon she didn't understand quite this well!"
- "Thanks, guys, I have a ride. That red convertible over there!"

Being a "Mature" Aunt—the Aunt's View

- "What do you mean, 'Is this my Grandchild?'"
- "I knew I shouldn't have stopped weight training."
- "I wonder if it's a good idea to get this much of a 'test-drive' of parenthood?"
- "What it amounts to is having three different sets of children."
- "Watching my Sister/Brother grow up once was enough. Who knew I'd be doing it all over with her/his children?"

Having a "Mature" Aunt—
the Niece/Nephew's View

- "She's kind of like a Mom, without all the rules."
- "Are you sure you had the same parents?"
- "Roller Blades, for me? Gee, thanks."
- "Mom/Dad actually takes you seriously, doesn't she/he?"
- "You mean you've actually got room for me and all my roommates?"

Though timing may be everything, you probably won't/didn't get to plan the timing of Aunthood or the age of your Aunts. And you probably will/did find that there's a lot to be said for Aunts both "underage" and "mature"— both being them and having them.

Aunts Who Aren't
Real Reasons/Honorary Titles

*T*he question is: "What makes an Aunt a *real* Aunt?" Since relatives happen largely by accident, being a "blood Aunt" doesn't automatically qualify you as "real." It also means that "honorary Aunts," the ones who get the title without having a genetic claim to it, are still in the running to be genuinely and absolutely "real."

If you've read the grown-up children's classic *The Velveteen Rabbit*, you know that it provides a test for what it is that makes someone real. That test, which has to do with time and availability and loyalty, could be applied to the matter of what makes an Aunt "real." Now, this doesn't mean that the Aunt, to use the book's example, has to have the fur loved off of her to become as real as the enduring skin horse. (Unless, of course, the Niece/Nephew is an avid animal rights activist. But, then, that's another matter.)

What it comes down to is that the Aunt, whether she got to be one by blood, proximity, or respect, isn't real just because she has the title. Like the characters in that children's classic, she *becomes* real by the painstaking process of being there.

Being there for the first teeth and the loss of them; for the first steps and the first ones taken—independently or defiantly—in a direction quite unlike what the adults would have planned for a particular Niece or Nephew. Being there when a nightmare marches too aggressively toward the world of waking. Being there when a Niece or Nephew is finding it so hard to believe that his or her Parents can actually have friends. Friends who actually understand them and can even explain them to their children, who are probably just standing too close to see them clearly.

Being there sometimes means being welcomed. But, it can't depend on that. Sometimes an Aunt's "being there" is a matter of having the spear-carrier role in the drama that is her Niece's or Nephew's star vehicle. She may sometimes be barely visible, but it's still important that she be there.

World-class "being there" includes sitting on hard benches at grammar school hockey games. And applauding at your tenth performance of *Our Town* as if you had never seen it before. And taking the grade school pageant about the parts of speech building a sentence as seriously as if you were the drama critic for the *New York Times* reviewing a new play by a Nobel Prize–winning playwright.

Sometimes the "being there" is best done passively, as when a Nephew or Niece just needs to vent and knows that he or she can count on you, later on, to have just as good a "forgetory" as you have a memory.

Other times the "being there" is best done actively, as when you attend a town meeting with a Niece or Nephew and show yourself unafraid to take a strong, even if unpopular, stand on an issue you both consider important.

An Aunt's "being there," when at its best, includes listening, laughing, remembering, forgetting, sympathizing, challenging, crying. It is sometimes expected to include (not necessarily in this order): shelter, transportation, ready cash, arbitration, hostage negotiation, fashion consultancy, relationship counseling, whimsy, academic guidance, and personnel and placement services.

And to the very end of her life, it means that the Aunt stands as a shield between her Niece or Nephew and his or her mortality.

A pretty impressive portrait, isn't it? But, the most impressive part of all is that it's drawn from life. Real memories, real stories. Real women, remembered by real men and women, boys and girls. Stop the videotape of your own memory, and explore the images that pop up as you read the descriptions of Aunts real and honorary. You may find the Aunts who, in your own life, became real. You may find women like some of these.

Cousin Helen was of an age to have been given the honorary title of Aunt, yet she was always known simply as Cousin Helen, which is what she was to my Father. Not the child-of-your-Aunt/Uncle kind of cousin, but rather Cousin in one of those distant ways that people discuss and keep track of only at family reunions. Cousin Helen played the piano. She had a canary whose cage had to be covered at night so that he would know not to sing. She wore dark glasses, even inside, which was unusual when I was a child, though it might not be today. But it was all right for her to wear dark glasses, because Cousin Helen was blind. And I thought she was a magician because she could feel pages that didn't have any visible words on them and know the words to a story. She had been able to see at one time, but an accident when she was a little girl had put her into a life-time of darkness. It was obvious, though, even to a child, that Cousin Helen's darkness was all on the outside of her. On the inside, she had her own sources of light, and there was enough to light up her life, her always bright and spot-less home, and the lives of her friends and family. Since she was an only child, that family comprised mostly Cousins, like my Father, but she was anything but peripheral in their lives. My Parents asked her to be the godmother of their youngest child, born as a surprising addition to the family when my Mother was forty-six years old. That is how I got a singular godmother who became an honorary Aunt of the kind called "Cousin." And whose courage and absence of self-pity qualified her as a "real" Aunt by even the most exacting standards.

Lucille was another of my Father's Cousins. But, she was the immediate kind, child of his Mother's Sister. As a con-temporary of our Parents, she had every reason to be called "Aunt Lucille" but never was. She was always just Lucille. And she was always there, for all her family. Her profession was career counseling. Her genius was getting people to recognize their own talents. Asking them the right ques-tions and then taking the time to listen. She also was an only child and never married. So, her contribution to her extended family was not to give it more members, but rather to give the current members of all ages the chance to know each other better than we ever would have without Lucille. Hers was the house where we gathered for family reunions. Hers was the will that remembered each of scores of Cousins with a modest bequest that gave them access to fulfilling one of their dreams—mine financed my first trip to Ireland. Hers was the living room that had boxes of View-Master slides to entertain visiting children while the adults conversed. (Proving that you don't have to give birth to children to understand them.) In the world of her living room, children could discover a wider world. She also mediated family disagreements, firmly guiding whole families to discover that they had more in common than they had differences. Lucille is a perfect example of all the very real Aunts who are never called by the title.

Aunt Julia was another matter. She was the lady who walked down a Dublin street the day that Irish-born singer-storyteller Carmel Quinn's Mother died and, from that moment, unceremoniously commenced to "be there" with her Nieces for good and always. Especially for "good." The multitalented entertainer (who burst on the scene as a teenaged regular on Arthur Godfrey's show) could fill an evening with stories of Aunt Julia. She was apparently a decidedly "real" Aunt, especially in her roles as defender of virtue and champion of all those people whose kindness stops short of "suffering fools gladly." "The medals" and "the hat" demonstrate those points.

Aunt Julia made it a point to give Carmel and her Sisters a large selection of religious medals and then to pin them to various pieces of their clothing—especially, and obviously not by coincidence, just before they went out on dates. If a young boy found himself overwhelmed and hands began to stray, it was sure that what he'd contact first would be a medal. Where Aunt Julia's actual "being there" ended, "the medals" began.

But, when it came to being there for people other than her Nieces, Aunt Julia had limits. "The hat" proves that premise. It seems she always made it a point to have a hat near at hand to be prepared for when the doorbell would ring. Whenever it did, she quickly placed her hat firmly on her head before answering the door. If the visitor was a known bore, she was dressed to say, "As you can see, I'm just on my way out, or I'd surely ask you to come in." Aunt Julia is a good example of the fact that there is nothing saccharine sweet about a real Aunt's "being there."

Great-Aunt Rebecca was, unfortunately, still on the cusp of the recent legalization of marijuana when she began to be troubled with a glaucoma-like condition. When she heard her doctor comment, offhandedly, that some people felt the smoking of marijuana could alleviate her symptoms, Becca displayed one of the qualities that mark an Aunt as "real" whether or not she is related by blood. The "real" Aunt demonstrates an ability to get the best from Nieces and Nephews by simply expecting it. Prompted by her, the Niece or Nephew can do what he or she never believed possible. In the case of Great-Aunt Rebecca, you could substitute "demanding" for "expecting" and "marijuana" for "the best." Here is how it happened.

Her Great-Niece was an actress, Becca reasoned, and was living in New York. So . . . "How hard could it be?" Becca would never be accused of being an Aunt who got too little from her Niece by expecting too little. She picked up the phone and began to put the wheels in motion. She was not one bit shy about asking for what she needed. But she was somewhat guarded in the language she used. In her conversations with her "worldly" Great-Niece, Becca was circumspect: "Just in case the authorities are listening." As a result, it took quite a while for the young actress to recognize the exact identity of the "vegetable" Becca was asking her to secure.

And so began a real-life chapter in what would pass for a Jimmy Breslin book. Niece began calling friends and asking how it was that one secured "vegetable." A "nice young man" was identified, and, because Becca found him to be up to her standard, he became her "vegetable" dealer. Before her death, Becca actually became highly opinionated on the varying quality of his continuing supply of "vegetable." And as she did, she also became a highly aromatic illustration of how futile it is to expect either Aunts or their Nieces to fit into stereotypes of their roles. For, there was the Great-Niece, occasionally laughing, occasionally anguishing over how to figure out whether Great-Aunt Becca was perhaps enjoying ill health a little too much. And what, if anything, she should do about it. Great-Aunt Becca may have started out being real in genetic terms, but it was her ability to get her Niece to exceed her wildest expectations of herself that truly marks her as an Aunt that would have been "real," whether or not she was related by blood.

Dressing the Part

S he may not be playing her part in a costume drama, but that doesn't mean that costuming is unimportant for the Aunt. There are practical matters to be considered. In the early days she'll want lots of pockets, very little graspable jewelry, and a strict code of "washables only."

There are other concerns as well. She may have wanted the part, but she doesn't necessarily want the image that sometimes goes with it. Clothes can't make the Aunt, but they can make her life in the role easier and, if she's smart, even slightly intriguing.

Wardrobe Tips for the New Aunt

*B*ecoming an Aunt for the first time is a little like climbing Everest. It goes much better if you wear the right clothes and have the right gear.

So, after you've given the baby shower and before the baby arrives, take a close look at your closets and your jewelry box and make sure you're prepared to dress for success as an Aunt. And don't listen to the cynics who suggest a bulletproof vest, flak jacket, waterproof bodysuit, and motorcycle helmet.

First Steps

1. Retire all silk shirts and dresses. Replace with machine-washable alternatives.
2. Retire all pierced earrings with any design element that can be used as a handle. (Or make friends with a plastic surgeon who repairs torn earlobes.)

3. Retire all clip-on earrings that can be ingested or that, by their bright color or shiny surface, constitute what officers of the courts could define as "an attractive nuisance."

4. Retire all large, sharp, shiny, or abrasive pins or brooches, especially ones worn on or near that shoulder on which a baby is burped.

5. Purchase vast quantities of Woolite, Wash 'N Dries, and Kleenex.

6. Retire all clothing with small, false, or purely ornamental pockets unsuitable for holding HandiWipes, Desitin, an extra diaper, and an absorbent hand towel.

7. If you require eyeglasses to fulfill such visually demanding tasks as reading the instruction panel on Baby Tylenol, buy a drawerful of these and put them in six to eight easy-to-remember, strategic locations. Abandon a chain or cord that allows you to hang eyeglasses around your neck. (Not only because it irrevocably brands you as "a person of a certain age," but mostly because it will almost certainly lead to the infant Nephew or Niece using said glasses as a platform on which to place his or her tiny feet and/or full weight. Or . . . to use the chain or cord to strangle either you or him/her or both!)

8. Reevaluate your wardrobe at each new developmental stage of the Niece/Nephew's life. When the baby begins to walk, retire all shoes not suited to running. Supplement pockets with fanny packs or other containers that can be attached to the body and into which vulnerable, cherished objects

made of china or crystal can be popped at a moment's notice.

9. When they reach the teen years, do your best to dress "down" so as not to induce in them the acute embarrassment of being seen with someone who is "hopelessly uncool."

10. Don't even dream of: smoking, failing to fasten your seat belt, or wearing the skin of any formerly living animal (or whatever may be the politically correct alternative of the day) from the moment the Niece/Nephew has his or her first "socially aware" teacher.

11. When the Niece/Nephew reaches soccer-playing age, invest in gloves, hats, and coats that protect against the elements but do not attract undue attention to the bleachers or sidelines. Favor padded coats that help an adult to withstand the rigors of long hours of sitting on unupholstered surfaces.

12. When the Niece/Nephew reaches marriage age, look around for a special-occasion outfit in beige or grey and take heed of the old maxim about the Mother of the Groom—that is, that "She should wear beige and say nothing." It's an even better rule for Aunts of the Groom.

Auntproofing

There are several reasons for needing to be "Aunt-proofed." It's not the fact of *being* an Aunt against which you need protection; it's the impression it gives. Be honest: when you see the man of your fantasies across the room, are you likely to rush to his side and say, "Hello, I'm Aunt Woman-You've-Been-Looking-for-All-Your-Life"? Not likely. So, what is the image (versus the reality) of an Aunt? Where did it come from? And how do you protect yourself from having it rub off on you?

General Advice for Aunts

Be aware that a great many images of Aunts come from nineteenth-century literature. So, for a lot of people, that word awakens the same sorts of impressions as words like "antimacassar," "machine" (used to describe a car), and "icebox" (used to describe a refrigerator). Quaintly old-fashioned versus stylishly retro. So, be alert to the fact that when your title is used, it just might conjure up those images. That's why you need to protect yourself and *Auntproof*.

Retroactive Auntproofing: Here's How It's Done

- If you have a ten-year-old automobile with 35,000 miles on the odometer . . . Hide it! If you have to go somewhere in public in it and someone discovers you starting to enter said car, look surprised, walk away from it murmuring, "Silly me," and hurry to stand next to the nearest low-slung, red, sleek, totally-impractical-looking one in the parking lot.

- If your fragrance is anything named Lavender or anything at all by Crabtree & Evelyn . . . shelve it for private use and replace it with one of the following:

  - One having a name that suggests danger, preferably one named after a lethal potion, a controlled substance, or a psychological malady
  - One with a decidedly under-forty image using initials and/or numbers for a name . . . or a part of speech or a geometric figure
  - A fragrance (preferably the sample vial distributed at an exclusive retailer) that only seriously affluent people could afford (and then only by taking a second mortgage on the penthouse)

- If you must serve dessert with a crust and a filling, be sure not to call it "pie." Try referring to it as *"tarte,"* making it as thin as possible, and garnishing it with nothing more caloric than paper-thin slices of even more fruit.

- If you own or are seen using a typewriter, make sure it's a fifty-year-old manual, and pretend that you're a tough city-room reporter on a metropolitan daily. You might try adding a fedora and a terminally wrinkled jacket just for good measure.

- If you must smoke, try to confine it to an occasional (large) cigar, enjoyed (highly visibly) while wearing a (very small) black dress.

- Go light on certain words used to describe positive experiences, such as: *delightful*, *scrumptious*, *groovy*, and *enchanting*. Better still, avoid all slang words, since they tend to become dated in a week. Fasten on the visual cues to understand what your Nieces/Nephews are actually saying. For example, "gross" is usually accompanied by the facial expression of one who has found a dead animal in the ventilation system; "co-ol" comes together with a look of unqualified approval; "bad" usually isn't, but what it *is* may not be clear, so say something like, "How bad is he/she/it?"

- When you hear your Nieces and Nephews say that an actor or actress is "smoking," don't assume that this has anything to do with the consumption of tobacco products. It means that the person is found to be, shall we say, remarkably attractive. Don't be drawn into a conversation that requires you to say who *you* think is "smoking." In general, deny all knowledge of performers who have not appeared in a hit film in the past seven years. When referring to those of an earlier box-office era, always preface the reference with the question, "Don't you love seeing his old films on AMC?"

Proactive Auntproofing: Here's How It's Done

- Keep your refrigerator looking as if it could be used as a bookshelf. Make sure that a quick peek into it will reveal nothing but virtuous supplies like spring water, fat-free yogurt, carrot and celery sticks, and the odd packet of sliced ginger.

- Establish modem connections to all your communications equipment. Try to act as if it is perfectly acceptable to be attached, umbilical-cord-style, to all the instruments of torture that ensure that you are never out of earshot of a phone or fax and never inaccessible to your clients, your family, and even your enemies.

- Own, or at least exhibit understanding of, a seemingly endless variety of activity-specific shoes. (Remember when a single pair of "sneakers" used to be enough?) Here are some suggestions: cross-training shoes, hiking boots, walking shoes, shoes for aerobics (high impact), shoes for aerobics (low impact), etc. You get the idea.

- Be sure to refer to the large, black disks that gave "disk jockeys" their name as "vinyls," not "records." Remember that records are what athletes set, not what music fans play on turntables. If you have a large collection of them, make it clear that you see them as a great investment in view of their antique status. Comment that you think CDs may soon be outmoded, soon to be replaced by DVDs.

- If the word *emoticon* is used, do not look blank and uncomprehending. These are the combinations of keyboard symbols such as punctuation marks, accents, and letters used by people who surf the Internet to convey (when viewed with the head sideways to the computer screen) emotions such as happiness—:-)—or sadness—:-(. Go a step further and remark that you are impressed with the Japanese invention of a new set of emoticons that can be viewed right side up. Your six-year-old Nieces and Nephews may not know the word *emoticon*, but they are very likely to know how to make them and what they mean.

- When introduced to a young woman you know to be married, do not ask if hers is a "maiden name" or a married one. Take it that (from the point of view of the woman you just addressed) it either doesn't matter or you don't need to know.

Suggested Contents: Auntproofed Refrigerator

1. Yogurt/plain/small container
2. Mineral water/still/large size
3. Cereal/Grape-Nuts or shredded wheat/small size
4. Fruit/long-life; for example, apples, oranges/3 each
5. Fruit/short-life; for example, fresh berries/half-pint
6. Bread/the grainier the better/small loaf/unsliced
7. Coffee/bean form/boutique brand/one-half pound
8. Capers/narrow bottle suitable for in-door storage
9. Fruit/social; lemons and/or limes/3 each
10. Margarine/tub versus stick-style/no-cholesterol
11. Sorbet/no sugar, no fat/1 pint (missing 2 tablespoons)
12. Beer/imported or from microbrewery/1 bottle

The Program Listing

*E*ven before the play begins, the audience can guess a lot about the characters by the way they're described in the playbill. So, it's important for the Aunt to make sure that her description fits the role. She may have to fight for her gerund, or consider when (and when not) to use her title. Aunts who are playing other roles at the same time have other concerns. Aunts, like movies, sometimes come as double features, and that means someone has to decide how they'll be billed.

You Oughta Have a Gerund

*T*he title of this chapter is meant to be sung—to the tune of "You Oughta Be in Pictures." And it's meant to be sung to Aunts. Because being an Aunt is about gerunds, even though no one talks about them anymore. I haven't heard "gerunds" used in a sentence since high-school Latin class when Sister Albertus explained that these were the "ing" words, like *being* and *loving* and *growing*, used to describe a generalized or uncompleted action.

But, while nobody is talking about gerunds these days, everyone is using them. Lately the noun *parent* has gotten a new life as a verb, "*to parent*" (the activity of being a Parent), and, more significantly, as a gerund. So, Parents are now covered in books and magazine departments on the subject of "Parenting," a word that recognizes that theirs is a role with a starting point but no ending. Using the word *Parenting* points out the fact that being a Parent is a continuing work in progress: something that, once it starts, never ends.

Which brings us to Aunts. Millions of people have an Aunt, probably several. There are as many millions of women who *are* Aunts and who think it's about time they got their fifteen minutes of fame. Like Parents, these people are also involved in *a continuing or not yet completed action*. Ask anyone who has seen her life change forever with the arrival of a Niece or Nephew. Aunts, like Parents, are forever. They too deserve to move from being nouns, to being verbs, to being gerunds: in other words, *The Day of Aunting* has arrived, providing the occasion to look back and forward, to celebrate Aunts of all eras. And that moves me to offer the following wisdom.

General Advice for Aunts

- Hold out for your gerund: you deserve one.

    Just as Parenting is a process that has a beginning but no end, so too is the lifelong adventure of being an Aunt. Anyone who thinks it has a tidy ending point has obviously never been an Aunt. Aunts who are satisfied just to be nouns have missed the fact that the minute someone becomes an Aunt, she becomes the star of a lifetime performance even though her role is support- ing player in the two-person drama that is a lifetime rela- tionship with a Niece or Nephew. It begins the moment that person is born and continues into the time when you both live only as memories. So, when you become an Aunt, you are really setting out on the unending road of Aunting.

What Does Aunting Include?

- Ceremonial Occasions—You are meant to be present (though not too obvious) at all family events involving your Niece or Nephew.

- Partnerships and Conspiracies—You will soon start hearing the words "I don't want to worry Mom or Dad, but I need to talk to someone . . . "; "We want to surprise Mom and Day on their anniversary, and we need some advice . . . but you can't tell."

- Cheerleading—Banish fears that you will be expected to qualify for the Dallas Cowgirls, but face up to the fact that you are expected to be a one-woman cheering section (traveling, when necessary) from the first neighborhood soccer game or kindergarten dance recital through the first Broadway opening and the wedding being held continents away.

- Commiserating—From the first "Stacy didn't invite me to her birthday party," to the latest, "How can I tell my parents that I didn't pass the bar?" you will be on call to use your special position of being close—but not too close—to the situation to be a good sounding board, or shoulder to weep on.

And What Should Aunting Exclude?

- Taking Sides
- Knowing It All

Aunts in Plain Brown Wrappers

*H*ave you noticed the *bracketing effect*? At first my Nieces and Nephews just called me "Annette." Then they began calling me "Aunt Annette" (or "Aunt Pop," or other arcane, family favorites). And then one day, when my oldest Nephew now towered over me, I noticed that he dropped the "Aunt," and I didn't argue the point. But, I didn't ask him why, so I'm left wondering.

I have one family of "Grands" who call me just plain "Aunt." (And don't let anyone tell you that isn't heartwarming.) I like to think it's because they see me as the very definition of Aunthood, the "Cher" of Aunts for whom one name is enough. But they are too young for me to ask, and so I'm left wondering.

The children of friends often call me Aunt because their Parents tell them to do so. These are balanced by friends' children whom I did not meet until they were adults and who *don't* call me Aunt. My college roommate's son, for instance, calls me "A," a nickname I had hoped would die when his Mother and I reached voting age. There are other people who make such a point of ensuring that their fully grown-up children call me Aunt that it makes me wonder whether there's a message, *not an entirely positive one,* in the title.

"To Aunt or not to Aunt," then, seems to be the question. And it might be open to just as many interpretations as Hamlet's "To be or not to be." Nieces and Nephews have their reasons why they do, or don't, use an Aunt's title. Aunts have their, often quite different, reasons for wanting or not wanting their title to be used. Parents have their reasons for urging their children to use or not use an Aunt's title. It begins to look as if there could one day be a college catalog listing an advanced sociology course entitled "The Aunt in Context: An exploration of the use of the title and what it reveals about the sociological structure of the extended family." The following lists, however, are offered on a strictly not-for-credit basis.

Times When an Aunt May Want to Use Her Title

1. *When stopped for speeding* . . . as in: "Because, Officer, my Nephew Danny just called me and said, 'Aunt Jean, Mom isn't home yet and the coach said that if I'm late for practice, he'll never let me play in Little League again.'"
2. *When her Nephew is stopped for speeding* . . . as in: "Because, Officer, my Nephew Danny was just asking me, "Do you think *this* is too fast, Aunt Jean?"
3. *When she's having an IRS audit* . . . as in: "Then I said, 'Children, how many times has Aunt Julie told you

not to use that box of receipts for making cutouts!'—but it was too late."

Times When She May Not . . .

1. *When she is being introduced to her Niece's urbane and sophisticated literature professor who just happens to look like Liam Neeson . . .* as in: "I'm Victoria's Aunt Ethel."
2. *On her office door . . .* as in: "It should be obvious."
3. *On her business card . . .* as in: (See above).

Times When an Aunt May Want to Hear Her Title Used

1. *When she has had six straight 14-hour days at work* and feels like a working machine and thinks the phrase "Get a life" is *not* funny.
2. *When she is being introduced to her Niece/Nephew's friends* and knows the title is being used to say, "You'll never believe it, but this cool human being—for an adult— is my *actual* Aunt."
3. *When it is used to accompany another title,* such as, "This is my friend, Aunt Barbara."

Times When She May Not . . .

1. *The day she has noticed her first wrinkle.*
2. *The day she has noticed her Niece/Nephew noticing her first wrinkle.*
3. *The day she gets her first unsolicited letter from the American Association of Retired Persons/AARP.*
4. *On all her "bad hair" days.*

Double-Feature
Aunts

*W*hat if the Aunt has another title? In England and other countries with monarchies this could, obviously, be a problem. But it holds for democracies too, because any country with press and other media tends to use lots of titles as well. Not ones connected with nobility, of course, but rather the kind that are used before or after the name, often set off by commas, to pinpoint that exact person and differentiate him or her from others who might share the same name. These titles are called *parentheticals* and are used to ensure that you will know that the subject under discussion is *Fred Astaire's dancing partner* Ginger Rogers, not Ginger Rogers the pet groomer, who lives next door. So, be prepared if you have a parenthetical and become an Aunt, or if you get an Aunt who has a parenthetical when you meet her. There are choices to be made. Will it be:

Aunt Queen Elizabeth
>   or
>   Queen Aunt Elizabeth?

Aunt Doctor Ruth
>   or
>   Doctor Aunt Ruth?

Aunt Attorney General Janet
>   or
>   Attorney General Aunt Janet?

Aunt First Lady Barbara/Hillary/Rosalyn
>   or
>   First Lady Aunt
>   Barbara/Hillary/Rosalyn?

Aunt Astronaut Sally Ride
>   or
>   Astronaut Aunt Sally Ride?

Aunt Pulitzer Prize–Winning Playwright Wendy
>   or
>   Pulitzer Prize–Winning Playwright
>   Aunt Wendy?

Aunt Talk Show Host Oprah/Rosie/Kathie Lee
>   or
>   Talk Show Host Aunt
>   Oprah/Rosie/Kathie Lee?

Aunt Country Music Star Reba
>   or
>   Country Music Star Aunt Reba?

A

Program
Note

As in On
(Versus Off)
A Pronouncing Guide Part I

ncle is not a particularly attractive word. Neither is *avuncular*, the adjective connected with it. But at least there's no doubt about how to pronounce it. Not so with *Aunt*.

Aunts should come with pronouncing guides. But since they don't, here are some pointers. You'll find others, ranging from "pond" to "picnic," scattered throughout the book, if the first doesn't work.

Pointers on How to Pronounce the Title

There are several schools of thought about how you pronounce the title of that female, qualified by blood, honor, or both to be called "Aunt." You have a dazzling array of choices. But before you make one, you should probably know the consequences and qualifications. Let's get "on" with the first possibility.

The Aunt as in On (Versus Off) Option

This pronunciation borrows the *o* the dictionary shows with
a single dot above it (ȯ). This is the one they show at the
bottom of the page next to the word *flaw*. Don't ask!

In this case you call her (or are called) Aunt=Ȯnt. (Don't
ask me why it isn't as in "flawnt"; I often find dictionaries
more challenging than the unknown words I look up in
them.)

If you were born in Britain and educated in its puzzlingly
titled "public schools"; or if you spent your childhood in
Muncie, Indiana, fantasizing that you had been; or if you
are obsessive about watching BBC television imports, this is
the one for you.

Consequences:

Be warned that you'll be giving your mouth, teeth, and lips
a workout if you use the Aunt = Ȯnt pronunciation and the
given name starts with a flat *A*, as in Ann. Try repeating five
times: Ȯnt Ann, Ȯnt Ann, Ȯnt Ann, Ȯnt Ann, Ȯnt Ann.
See what I mean? On the other hand, if she's called Olive
this is definitely the pronunciation for you (and probably
for her too).

If you use the Aunt = Ȯnt pronunciation to refer to the
scientific study of Aunts, namely *Auntology*, people may misunderstand and think you are talking about a particularly
arcane branch of philosophy devoted to the study of "being"
and called *ontology*. Whereas, of course, *Auntology* is instead
about the much more rewarding study of which this book
is the prime example.

Learning the Part

There ought to be a "Stanislavsky Method" for the Aunt. It's not good enough for her just to have gotten the part. Now she has to become the part. So, where does the Stanislavsky-less Aunt look to find her "inner identification" with her part? She could survey the cast and potential audience members to find out how they'd like to see it performed. She could look at how other people played it. She could take her cue from the special needs of the other actors. She could apply her life experience and even offer advice to others about how to make the role work for them. There are a lot of options, and she needs to get busy evaluating them. In the process—who knows?—she could even become the Stanislavsky of Aunting!

Role Model Roll Calls

*J*f Aunts made lists of the Aunts they'd like to *be*, and their Nieces and Nephews made lists of Aunts they'd like to *have*, you might be surprised how different those lists would be.

What it comes down to is that you can't get to *be* an Aunt by wishing. Nor can you *get* to have an Aunt that way. But, that still doesn't stop you from making "wish lists." Aunts do it. So do Nieces and Nephews. As you will see from some of the lists that follow.

Aunts You'd Like to Be

Auntie Mame (played by Rosalind Russell)
Auntie Em in *The Wizard of Oz*
Aunt Eller in *Oklahoma!*

Auntie Mame (played by Angela Lansbury)
Aunt Augusta (in *Travels with My Aunt*)
"Aunt Shirley" MacLaine
"Aunt Wendy" Wasserstein
Aunt March (at the *end* of *Little Women*)
Aunt Jessica Fletcher
Aunt Jemima
Aunt Martha Stewart

Aunts You'd Rather Not Be

Auntie Mame (played by Lucille Ball)
Miss Havisham in *Great Expectations*
"Aunt Leona" Helmsley
Howard Stern's Aunt
"Aunt LaToya" Jackson
"Aunt Lizzie" Borden
Aunt March (at the *beginning* of *Little Women*)
Aunt Calamity Jane
Aunt Princess Margaret of Great Britain

Aunts You'd Like to Have

Daisy Fuentes
Sandra Bullock
Whoopi Goldberg
Rosie O'Donnell
Barbie
Cindy Crawford
Mrs. FAO Schwarz
Whitney Houston

Kate Capshaw (Mrs. Steven/as in Dreamworks)
   Spielberg
"Auntie Pamela" Anderson Lee
Mrs. Fields
Mrs. Claus
Mrs. Hershey (as in candy)

Aunts You're Glad You Didn't Have

Aunt Marge Simpson
Aunt Cruella deVil
Aunt Joan Crawford
Aunt Marie Antoinette
Aunt Lady Godiva (*not* as in candy)
Aunt Carrie Nation
Aunt Eva Braun
Aunt Lucrezia Borgia
Aunt Lady Macbeth
Aunt Dorothy Parker
Aunt Wicked Witch of the East
Aunt Griselda (as in *Cinderella*)
Aunt Joan Collins
Aunt Amy Vanderbilt (as in etiquette)
Aunt Avid Vegetarian
Aunt Gloria (avidly anti-sugar) Swanson

On the other hand, there are points on which there is
unanimity.

Things Every Aunt and Her Nieces/Nephews Wish She Had

A huge discount at Toys "Я" Us

A self-cleaning van

Earplugs

A hotel (with twenty-four-hour room service) for sleep-overs

A degree in psychotherapy

Training as a negotiator

More Nieces and Nephews (on a "quick visit" day)

Fewer Nieces and Nephews (on a "sleep-over" night)

Stock in McDonald's/Burger King/Wendy's

A live-in cook

Stock in The Gap/Nike

A box for all hometown major-league baseball games

Season tickets to Chicago Bulls games

An instant casting service for perfect prom dates

Legally secured advance copies of all SAT exams

Opinion Poles

*I*t starts in the hospital. You return from the viewing window of the nursery. The Parents who have just worked so hard to give you a new Niece or Nephew look at you while in a dramatic state of vulnerability and ask, "Do you really think he/she is cute?" That's the beginning of a life that would challenge the world's most experienced diplomat. But it's all in a day's work for anyone ascending to Aunthood.

Aunts will find their opinions being sought, almost from the beginning. It is relatively easy to think of humane answers to the "Do you really think he/she is cute?" question, even if the new person in your lives is not—not yet, at least—notable for standard good looks. It gets tougher when that infant develops into someone who asks his or her own questions; tougher still when the Parents ask a set of questions in one ear and the Niece/Nephew asks those same questions in the other. "Do you think I/he/she should have an ear or an eyebrow or a navel pierced for the first/second/third time?" It is both a science and an art to know when and how to respond to those requests for an Aunt's opinion. Unless you're careful, these opinion polls can turn into opinion *poles* that leave you in your own personal "No Aunt's Land" with enemies on either side.

An Aunt's Treasury of Diplomatic Replies . . .

Author's Note: You may ask why all these replies reveal a certain, alleged Irish predisposition to answer a question with another question. To which the author answers, "Why not?"

. . . to Parents' Questions

- Could you have predicted how Denzel/Gloria would look when he/she was a newborn?
- Wouldn't you love to know what he/she will look like at our age?
- What would *you* want him/her to wear to the prom?
- Did you feel this way about other boys/girls he/she has dated?
- Are his/her classmates also planning to live in those apartments?
- Was anyone else in the family named Chrysanthia?

. . . To Nieces'/Nephews' Questions

- Have you made a list of the pros and cons of body piercing?
- What else were you considering wearing to the prom?

- Won't a biker cut feel very cold this winter?
- Did your parents like Tom/Mary right from the start? (Only use this one if you already *know* the answer.)
- Is that the hat your Mother admired the other day at the mall?
- Can the car run without a transmission?
- Do you know the driving age in Greece/North Dakota/Finland? (Only use this one if you don't *care* what the answer is.)
- What do you call that sort of shoe?

How to Recognize the Niece/Nephew of a Diplomatic Aunt

An Aunt's diplomacy in action eventually rubs off on Nieces/Nephews. You'll recognize that this is starting to happen when you sense that your Nephew/Niece has an impulse to ask one of these questions and then instantly rejects that impulse:

- Well, do you agree with me or with Mom and Dad?
- Should I just not tell Mom and Dad?
- But, can I while I'm staying with you?
- Are you *very* old?
- Couldn't you put me on *your* car insurance?
- What's wrong with hang gliding?
- Who's your favorite Niece/Nephew?

How to Recognize a **Really** Diplomatic Aunt

While waiting for the Aunt's diplomacy to rub off on her Nieces/Nephews, suppose one of those "never ask" questions actually gets asked. This is how the real pro answers them, demonstrating that kindness and diplomacy do not rule out firmness and honesty.

- Well, do you agree with me or with Mom and Dad?
  The important thing is that you believe in your position and that you are willing and able to explain why you do.

- Should I just not tell Mom and Dad?
  Only if you can do so and know that you will never regret it.

- But, can I while I'm staying with you?
  Geography isn't the issue; principle is. Don't ask me to take responsibility for your decisions.

- Are you *very* old?
  The important thing is that I'm not too old. The only people who are too old are the ones who have stopped learning, and I haven't.

- Couldn't you put me on *your* car insurance?
  Of course, if you're prepared to pay the difference that would make on my premiums.

- What's wrong with hang gliding?
  For the spectators, which I would be, there's no proportion between the risks and the rewards.

- Who's your favorite Niece/Nephew?
  The one that would know me well enough to know that I spend my energy learning to value people for who they are.

Think of Mame, Not Miss Havisham

*T*hink of the most glamorous Aunt you know. Quickly!

Now you see the problem.

There was a time when no one could imagine mentioning the words "glamorous" and "Grandmother" in the same sentence. Then Marlene Dietrich's daughter gave birth, and when they heard a Grandmother singing "Falling in Love Again" in that legendary, throaty voice, people had to reassess their preconceived notions of "Granny."

There are people out there who've done a lot to bring the image of Aunts from the era of Dickens to the age of the Internet. Maybe one of them could be *our* Marlene Dietrich. Not just glamorous, but a real '90s-type who, if she does not "have it all," at least has some of the most important parts of it. Who will be the World Poster Person for Aunts? And why?

Poster Woman for Aunts: The Aunts' Candidates

Think of what E.T. did for Reese's Pieces. No wonder the manufacturer fell in love with that candy-loving little extraterrestrial. Aunts would feel no less enthusiasm if certain high-visibility women would do us all the favor of, first of all, being Aunts, and then of talking a lot about the challenges and rewards of Aunting. The image campaign for Aunts would also be helped by what the Nieces/Nephews of these poster women said about them. It would suddenly not seem to be outside the realm of possibility to have Aunts who were "best of breed" in a number of the categories in which Aunts are expected to play a positive role.

Oprah Winfrey Think of what this candidate could do for the reputation of Aunts as people who encourage Nieces/Nephews to talk about what matters to them. To say nothing of their reputation for having available budget to offer unsecured loans.

Mame Dennis She may not be real, but the fictional Auntie Mame lent her name to the language and became a synonym for Aunts who combine flamboyance with a conscience and a heart.

Wendy Wasserstein This playwright has made it clear that an Aunt can be funny, hip, and hugely accomplished. And she's even written a book about her Niece. (Which makes her only negative the fact that she might give other people's Nieces and Nephews artificially elevated expectations.)

Shirley MacLaine Proving that Aunts are limber of mind as well as of body, this candidate offers the benefit of being able to represent several different centuries, all at one time.

Sandra Day O'Connor Talk about being able to arbitrate intrafamily disputes! This Supreme Court justice is just the ticket to polish an Aunt's desired image as "fair and wise."

Barbra Streisand Since the connection between teen Nieces/Nephews and their collections of CDs is closer than that between paper and ink, how great would it be to have an Aunt-figure with this many platinums to her credit? With an Aunt Barbra in their lives, could a permanent discount at Barnes & Noble Records be far behind? And as she herself might say, "It couldn't hurt" at the movie box office either.

Ricky Lauren Shopping is supposed to rank high on the Niece/Nephew's list of "Things I like to do with my Aunt." It would take on a whole new luster if the relative in question were Mrs. Ralph Lauren. She could also personify the Aunt's supposed ability to answer all questions asked while the Niece/Nephew is in panic mode on matters of good taste in wardrobe and home decor.

Donna Karan Clothing and Aunts go together in most people's chains of associations. From the layette onward, she is often the giver of gifts that can be worn. There is, of course, a period when the Niece/Nephew goes through the "Oh, yuck, not clothes!" stage, greeting gifts in that category as equal in appeal to, say, a snow shovel or slide rule. The stage is short, however, and replaced by one lasting for most of the rest of life. So, imagine, if for that long haul, the fashion guru were Aunt Donna. Equally adept at making males and females look their ever-so-chicly understated best (and with the added ability to make them and their homes smell better), this poster woman would banish forever the nasty rumor that Aunts give gifts that are square or quaint or otherwise undesirable.

Martha Stewart Once you're over the initial intimidation of having anyone in the family who is so uncomfortably close to being competent at *everything*, think of how Nieces/Nephews would warm to the possibility of having someone at the other end of the phone whom they could ask every question they could ever have about general entertaining (as in "They're arriving for dinner in eight minutes and what am I supposed to say if they ask, 'Where at the table would you like us to sit?'"), menu planning, and landscaping. Besides, it would do wonders for the Aunt's supposed ability to have an answer for anything if there were an Aunt who could, without missing a beat, describe exactly how to stencil fall leaves on table napkins.

Celine Dion As the youngest in a family the size of hers, she just has to be a multiple Aunt. Imagine what it would do for the rest of the Aunts out there if she were to drop a remark that the first thing she does when a new album appears is to autograph advance copies for her Nieces and Nephews and all their friends.

Mary Higgins Clark Picture a circle of adolescents gathered around a campfire telling scary stories, each wondering what to say when his or her turn comes around. Each of them knows that all the others will already know all the *Goosebumps* scenarios. But, what if one person in that circle were known to have an Aunt whose murder mysteries perennially put her at the top of the best-sellers list? It could only serve to raise the stock of Aunts in general if this candidate were to suggest that she got most of her best plots from previewing the ideas for her Niece or Nephew. And it might add motivation to listen a little more carefully when any Aunt tells a story.

Rosie O'Donnell With seven actual Nieces and Nephews (at this writing), the woman a national magazine dubbed "The Queen of Nice" is a natural choice. Suited by temperament and armed with an endless supply of koosh balls, Ring-Dings, a platform for airing Niece's and Nephew's jokes, and winning answers for every game of Trivial Pursuit, this candidate has all the qualifications.

Adopting a New Way of Seeing the World

The title for this chapter heading could be punctuated in two entirely different ways and still make sense:

1. *Adopting a New Way of Seeing the World*
   or
2. *Adopting: A New Way of Seeing the World*

Both of them are equally true. In the life of the Aunt, a whole new world opens with the birth of a person who becomes her Nephew or Niece. Once that happens, the world is simply never the same and she never again sees it exactly the same way.

What follows, though, is about the second punctuation. It's about the very special role of being an Aunt to someone who is adopted, and it is directed to the women who have had or may in the future have that honor.

If your Niece or Nephew happens to have been birthed by someone you do not know and then adopted by someone you do, the magic of Aunthood is only heightened. And if you come from a family that has not experienced adoption before, then the coming of your adopted Niece and/or Nephew is a double revelation, equivalent to seeing your first feat of magic performed by Houdini. This sort of event is powerful stuff. Because you get to experience not just the birth of a child, but also the literal birth of a bond.

For any Aunt, there is a magical moment of getting to see how that new Niece or Nephew brings to the world a fresh variation of the theme of its Parents' genes. As the Aunt of an adopted Niece or Nephew you exchange that moment for a whole new set of insights and discoveries.

Isn't He/She Just Like . . .

First of all, you get a chance to get cured of the "comparison disease." Muddling through the heady experience of seeing a new personality evolve is not for sissies. You need to be resolutely original, uncompromisingly willing to be surprised. The big temptation is to take refuge from all that newness and hide behind the nearest cliché. When you are amazed/dismayed/elated at the way your Nephew or Niece looks, acts, solves problems, laughs, walks, bargains . . . whatever . . . the easy way is to fall back on what you heard people say when you were the new one in other people's lives. Remember how often you heard things like this: "She's just like Aunt Maggie," or, "That temper is the Maher side of her," or, "All the Dohertys have those blue eyes" ("Aren't mine at least a tiny bit distinctive," you wondered), or, "You must sing. How could Peggy's sister not be a singer?" or, worst of all, "There's no use trying to teach mathematics to a Cunningham."

People are so afraid of being surprised. They're so hungry to find a formula that will neutralize the profound unpredictability of life.

The great thing about the adopted members of families is that, in spite of all people's efforts to fit them into preconceived mental molds, they get a better-than-average chance to be and to become themselves. Since most members of the family will know little or nothing about the biological Parents of this new person, they know they'll look pretty feeble if they haul out all the old chestnuts about the adopted boy or girl being/acting/looking/reacting "Just like so and so."

Remember "So and So"? They're those Tweedledums and Tweedledees of family history who gradually come to take on the force of myth by being referred to so often. The danger they pose is that, if taken seriously, they can rob the person who is likened to "So and So" of his or her incomparable individuality. In the sweep of generalization, the uniqueness of individuals, especially new, young individuals, can be brushed under the carpet, leaving the child to be endlessly compared to some other member of the extended family. The wonderful gift of the adopted Nephew or Niece is that his or her uniqueness can't be simply brushed off in the sweep of generalizations about heredity traits. This is unquestionably an advantage for the adopted person, but it can also be a great and abiding lesson for you as his or her Aunt. You can apply the lessons learned in relation to your adopted Nieces/Nephews to becoming wary of drawing too rapid or too general conclusions about related-by-blood Nieces/Nephews as well.

Aunts, Choice, and Adoption

It is obvious that Parents of adopted children have those children in their lives by choice. There are no "accidental" adoptions. That element of choice is one of the great bonds between adoptive Parents and the Aunts they inherit or adopt for those children. This may be especially clear in the case of the honorary (why not say "adopted"?) Aunts that Parents choose for their adopted children. But even for Aunts-by-blood, the real connection between an Aunt and her Nephews and Nieces is the fact that they choose to share life's experiences.

Aunts are rarely charged with desertion. It is clear that when they are in the lives of Nieces and Nephews, they are there by choice. Even when they come to their status as Aunts by the accident of birth, it is the big decision to carve out a special place in their lives for a Niece or Nephew that is the birth of the Aunt's bond to that person. The coming of an adopted child is a great reaffirmation of the truth that the power of choice creates connections every bit as lasting and as powerful as blood.

You only-children who become honorary Aunts to adopted children can truly be kindred spirits to your adopted Nieces and Nephews. Who could have more credibility than you in reassuring your Nieces and Nephews, for the rest of their lives, that choice is, without a doubt, as strong a cement as genes in forging the ties between people. And for all the world's "honorary" Aunts, only-children or not, your adopted Nephews and Nieces are living reminders of the fact that being an "honorary" Aunt is a singular honor indeed; the honor of being chosen.

Aunts, Lamaze, and Adoption

Before the adopted Niece or Nephew arrives into the life of your family or friends, you'll find yourself wishing that there were some sort of Lamaze course for adoptive Parents and their extended circle of relatives and friends. The people who really need the guidance and conditioning represented by these birthing preparation classes are the ones who will become Parents by adoption. Whether they adopt through an agency or take on the challenging/rewarding/demanding task of private adoption, they spend months and even years of facing extraordinary new demands. While the changes that engulf them may not be as obvious as the physical changes of pregnancy, they are going through a process every bit as challenging. And unlike the "couples-only" system of Lamaze, the adoptive Parents really need an extended network to cushion all the impact they will experience at every step of the long and demanding way.

As the prospective Aunt to the adopted, you may find that you should start your Aunting activities well in advance and be willing to be a sort of Lamaze coach for the unpregnant. While one set of prospective Parents needs to have a coach for breathing, the others probably need the most practice in listening. So, in this pre-Aunthood period, work with the expectant Parents on the art of listening. And, for that matter, work with them equally hard on the fine points of not listening.

For example, maybe just by listening to the conversations with various prospective birth Mothers that they recount, you can help them learn how to listen to a birth Mother and hear whether she has reached a point of decision. You may be able to help them find how to take her with ultimate seriousness and yet not expect more of her than she is able to give. They need to learn the challenging art of growing close enough to that birth Mother to gain her confidence and hear her hopes for her unborn child, while remembering that she will very likely want to sever that relationship once the child for whom they share concern has been born. An Aunt stands a good chance of knowing something about that special combination of closeness and separateness.

It is also quite possible that the Aunt can help the prospective Parents of an adopted child screen out the heedless remarks of people who miss the point of what their search for their child really means.

These are the possibly well-meaning but definitely insensitive people they meet in the supermarket who hear of their search and say things like, "Adopting? Oh, you're getting your baby the easy way." It may be a bit easier for you, the prospective Aunt, to empathize and help them put at a safe distance such knee-jerk reactions of people who don't understand adoption. Perhaps you can share some of the skills you have developed in dealing with the same sort of people who have said to you, "Well, at least it's easier for you to deal with his disappointment at not making the team/being accepted by the school/getting the job/being dumped by his fiancé, since you're *only* the Aunt."

And you can help those about-to-adopt Parents learn how and where to listen. Remind them of the insights of people like the great anthropologist Richard Leakey in his book *Origins Reconsidered: In Search of What Makes Us Human*. There he notes that the brains of most mammals are "finished" before they are born. And he points out that, by contrast, the brain of the human child goes on developing for at least nine months after its birth. That is great good news to adoptive Parents who may fleetingly regret the fact that their child may have no prenatal memory of the sound of their voices. Fortunately, there is still time to forge those extraordinary links. With all due respect to anthropologists, it's quite possible that you, as an Aunt, are better prepared than even the greatest of them to remind the prospective Parents of your adopted Niece or Nephew that there is every reason to be optimistic that rare bonds can continue to be invented long after that child's birth. That is, after all, just the sort of optimism you are developing as you await the arrival of your adopted Niece or Nephew.

Where's Aunt Waldo?

Useful Advice for the High of Profile

There's a certain "Where's Waldo?" quality to life as an Aunt. You know Waldo, that little cartoonlike character who is always shown packed in among masses of people. You're sure he's there, but you're not certain exactly where. The game is to find him.

The Waldo factor in the life of the Aunt is similar. Think about it. Do you doubt that Aunts have traveled in space? Fought in wars? Won Nobel Prizes? Pulitzer Prizes? Oscars? Grammys? Any doubt that they drive trucks? Pilot planes? Run corporations? Do brain surgery? Win Olympic medals? With the possible exception of the Vatican, it's probably pretty likely that there is at least one Aunt in every corridor of power. It's just that they're not visible *as Aunts*. That's the secret. And it can be a really useful secret, especially to people who might be suffering from being a little too high-profile. Which leads to offering what could be some useful . . .

. . . *Advice from Aunts for the High of Profile*

Simpson Juror (at any past, present, and/or future trials) Don't fight your way through the flashbulbs—just introduce yourself as someone's Aunt. You may not get a book contract, but your life will be a lot less harrowing. When cornered by an aggressive reporter, insist upon talking about your Nieces/Nephews.

Carolyn Bessette-Kennedy With the designation "New wife of the person often described as 'the world's sexiest man,'" what could you expect? But don't despair. Help is at hand, right there on the family tree. Tap into the one resource that will yield you some longed-for privacy. There must be dozens of people qualified to call you Aunt Carolyn. Make sure that they do. And be sure to introduce yourself that way . . . "Hi, I'm Rose's Aunt," for example. It may not afford complete protection from the paparazzi, but it could very likely help.

FBI Informer Before the Bureau and the taxpayers lay out a fortune to buy you a new identity and put you in a witness protection program, consider this possibility. Have an agent take you to a family wedding of your choice (even one in your own family) and introduce you all around as a long-lost Aunt of the groom. You'll be amazed at how securely unrecognized you'll begin to feel. And if you want to feel really secure in your anonymity, just produce a booklet of childhood photos of the groom and offer to tell the "really charming little story" behind each one. You'll be as good as gone!

Lottery Winner From the moment you told the world those winning numbers were yours, it probably seems that there has been a phone call or solicitation for every one of the gazillion dollars coming to you. Worthy causes are coming out of the woodwork. So, how do you discourage them without winning a reputation as the *Czarina of Mean?* Just tell every television, radio, and print reporter that you are the Aunt of several dozen worthy but penniless Nieces and Nephews, all of them earnest if not gifted students with fond dreams of attending Ivy League colleges.

Political Candidate You're in the race. You wanted to be. But, what you didn't want was the laser beam of public scrutiny. The seemingly endless appetite for any bit of seemingly irrelevant information about you. As any Aunt can tell you, you need to get on to a different playing field. Get smart. Have new posters made saying, "Vote for Aunt Kay!" Pepper your stump speeches with anecdotes about your Nieces and Nephews. When your opponent one-ups you in a debate, make him or her look heartless by recounting how your concerns for your siblings' children and those of your friends compel you to take the positions you have on (fill in the blank). Put your opponent in the position of being forced to say, "I disagree with *Aunt* Kay." And, if all else fails, insist on having your Nieces and Nephews accompany you on every television appearance or interview. You may not be handled with kid gloves, but they probably won't be boxing gloves, either. And who knows, you might even win the election.

Rehearsing with the Cast

It's a play, after all, not just a monologue or dramatic reading. So, the Aunt doesn't really know what her role is until she starts working with the other members of the cast. Her success in the role depends on them. She starts to listen for what their lines imply as well as what they literally state. She spends time getting to know how her lines sound to them. She realizes that she's in a kind of "cosmic buddy system" in which everyone has to be able to count on each other. She knows what she never wants to hear from the other cast members and what they never want to hear from her. She realizes that this is no "part-time" role and that she's in it for the long haul. In other words, she really gets to know the meaning of the phrase "ensemble performance."

Being of Sound Mind

There were some perilous moments before my (blood and honorary) Nieces and Nephews started reaching twenty-one when both my Sister and her husband and a good friend and her husband had designated me, in their wills, as the guardian of their children in the event of their deaths. In other words, in addition to the loss of my dearest friends, I also faced the possibility of becoming the single, working Mother of seven children, all living with me in a studio apartment in New York City. This is a threat that got my attention! And that now moves me to give some further . . .

. . . General Advice to Aunts

- Beware of compliments that come with big price tags. Your Sister/Brother and their respective spouses say you have the most/best influence on their children and so they wish to name you, in their wills, as guardian of their children in the event that "anything happens to us."

What to Do When They Want to Name You Guardian

Approach Number One

Do everything in your power to ensure that the aforementioned "anything" never happens.

Some For Instances

- Throw your body in front of your sibling and spouse if they ever undertake a journey more complicated than a trip to the supermarket, *together*.

- Cut out and mail to said couple all advertisements offering discounts for singles traveling as singles (these are very hard to find). Failing this, make a compelling scrapbook of destinations reachable by foot, and work hard to sell them as well-known romantic turn-ons for siblings who travel with spouses.

- Study the actuarial tables and familiarize yourself with all perilous forms of work, transportation, and recreation. If the sibling/spouse must indulge in any of these, encourage them to do so only when accompanied by all their children.

- Invest time and energy in preventive mental health for sibling and spouse; keep them laughing—it's supposed to be very therapeutic and extend life.

Approach Number Two

Participate in the estate-planning session and making sure that certain minimum standards are met in the provisions being made for Aunt/guardian and her newly enlarged family.

Some For Instances

• A mortgage-free dwelling with a minimum of one bedroom and one bath per child willed to the Aunt.

• A (generous!) trust fund for each child willed to the Aunt.

• A nanny (willing to work weekends) for each child willed to the Aunt.

Five Tactics for Discouraging the Willing of Children to the Aunt

1. Remark that whether children grow up to be saints or serial killers is all a matter of nature, not nurture.
2. Declare that Hitler would probably have been no better if he had been hugged a lot as a child.
3. Defend the actions of guardians of child stars who were discovered to have raided their trust funds.
4. Make it known that you favor a "gone equals forgotten/out-of-sight-out-of-mind" attitude toward the departed.
5. Demonstrate an inability to remember the children's names and/or tell them apart.

What to Do When All Else Fails

Buy yourself a video camera and prepare for an interesting but totally unpredictable future.

Topics for the Conversation

*Y*ou could actually say that the whole relationship between Nieces/Nephews and their Aunts is one big lifetime conversation. So, it's a good idea to put some effort into making sure it's an interesting one. And that takes a combination of work and imagination and figuring out what life looks like from the other partner's side of the conversation. As the Aunt, you've probably been conversing longer, so you'd better take the lead. If you take special care to get it right in the earliest days of your relationship with your Niece or Nephew, before the world at large even believes it's possible to converse, the conversations of the rest of your shared life will take care of themselves. Meantime, it may be useful to have a sort of "starter kit" of advice on establishing good habits of Aunt-to-Niece-or-Nephew conversation.

Some Advice to Aunts

- "My, what a big girl/boy you're getting to be!" is a definite loser. A real conversation squelcher. Unless the Niece/Nephew has grown several feet since the last meeting—and is glad to have done so—there simply isn't a lot more to say after that kind of an opening.

- So is, "What's new?" I remember being thrown into a panic when I heard these words booming from one of our country "Uncles," whose voice was great at calling cattle in from the field but more than a little intimidating to a person less than three feet tall. For a person with only the vaguest idea of time and no sense at all of what would be considered new to a person who seems remarkably *old*, that's the kind of question that is likely to generate only silence, not conversation.

- If there's one message you want to get across to your Nieces/Nephews it's that each of them is absolutely unique, a never-before, never-again kind of miracle. So, try to make your conversations as specific as they are. Children have radar that detects vagueness and generalities, long before they know what those words mean. The tiniest child knows the difference between being focused on versus fawned over, and knows that one is desirable and the other is not.

- It's a good idea to start at the very beginning to avoid talking down to this person who will be in your life for a long time to come. That doesn't mean you talk about the stock market to a six-month old, or exchange recipes with a toddler. It just means that you make an effort to find out where that person is at any given moment and then start the talking at that point.

Topics of Conversation with Infants

Before concluding that it is impossible to have a conversation with an infant, just remember that there is a moment in every conversation when a statement develops into a dialogue. When really good conversation happens it is probably because care has been taken at that early stage to listen, to observe, and to find the common ground that will be able to support both sides of the shared talk. So, think of the preconversational conversations with an infant Niece/Nephew as the warm-up for the continuing verbal exchanges of a lifetime. In general, a good conversation begins when one person tunes in on the big/important/valued topic in the other person's life. For infants, that topic is, very definitely, discovery. So, focus in on some of the really central discoveries.

Smells This is the only way infants distinguish one thing or person from another for the first days of their lives. So, try some opening gambits like these:

> *"That's the smell of grass that's just been cut. When you start recognizing colors you'll know it as the green stuff growing outside your window. The day will come, sooner than we both imagine, that you will be wanting to run barefoot in it, or are being asked to mow it."*

By the time you've said all that, the tiny person you are addressing will have caught on to the fact that you are talking to him or her and will be responding. Don't expect to understand the response. Maybe the child is expressing relief that someone is saying something that sounds much realer than the stream of baby talk and clucking sounds he or she usually hears from adults. But whatever the sounds mean, enjoy them and recognize that a dialogue has begun that will go on for a lifetime.

Sounds This subject is another winner in a baby's life, but remember, when it comes to sounds, more is not always better. Sounds need to be soothing. So, try:

> *"I'll bet my voice reminds you of your Mother's/ Father's. That's because we're what's called siblings. We had the same Mommy and Daddy, so we have lots of things in common.*

Or try:

> *"Listen to this: it's a song that was popular when your Parents and I were in high school. I never thought of it as a lullaby then, but then I never thought about you then, either. So, let's give it a try and see if you think it's music to sleep by." (The good news is that as long as it's soft and soothing, the infant is not too picky about its being on key, or including the right words.)*

Stream of Consciousness The best icebreakers for those first few moments of talking to your Niece/Nephew are ones about which they feel some passion. At first, it is likely to be the recent, big attention-getter: being born. It is obviously the biggest thing in the small person's recent past. So, consider:

"Everyone is so glad that you came. It must all seem so strange out here, and it can't have been easy to get here. But there are so many people who are glad to see you and will try to make you welcome."

So, whatever the subject, these early conversations can be an invaluable way of establishing the lifelong ground rules that will govern the spoken parts of your lifetime relationship to your Nieces and Nephews. The subjects will change, but the pattern of expressing interest in what matters to that Niece or Nephew will always succeed in bringing you closer.

But There Aren't Any Unicorns

Aunts and Faith

*I*t happened one day while playing "What is it?" with one four- and one six-year-old Nephew. The objective of this game is to select some object at hand, ask, "What is it?," and then proceed to assign it really wacky identities. We had a sock with so big a hole in its toe that it was really just a fabric tube. Of course, there's absolutely no question of saying, "This is a sock with a big hole in the toe." As the saying goes, "No way!" If you say something literal and unimaginative like that, you are definitely the loser.

So, I said, "It's a muffler for a unicorn." I thought that was a pretty good entry. What happened next set me to thinking about Aunts and faith.

"But there's no such thing as unicorns," six-year-old Neddie said.

"Are you sure?" I countered.

Silence.

"Are there dragons?" I asked.

"Yes," the answer came back instantly.

"Where? In your yard? In the hotel lobby?"

"Of course not, silly!"

"Then, where?"

"In my book . . . in movies."

"But did you ever see one . . . *in person?*"

"Well, no . . . but . . . "

"Then . . . why not a unicorn?"

When dealing with people of six or of four, it's important to know when to make an issue of something and when not to. So, why the big deal about unicorns? Something tells me it's an issue of faith. And one of the things Aunts are often called on to be is "defenders of faith." Not the religious kind of faith, mind you. Since that kind of faith is a gift, there's no use defending it. Just unselfconsciously savor your own gift, if you're lucky enough to have it; hope that your Niece or Nephew may receive his or her own gift; and get on with helping them understand how much faith there is in everyday life, and help make them be brave and balanced and humorous enough to exercise it.

Think about it. Every time you walk into a building, you have to take it on faith that its outsides are still there while you're inside.

For all of us who are part of the group of people born before 1970, we are constantly called upon to exercise faith in relation to the computer, which is, we are asked to believe, our friend. We must take it on faith that it is storing the words we labored so hard to write and that it will not, later, hide them from us by some malicious turn of electronic malevolence.

As members of the culture of "plastic," we have to believe that the person who takes our credit cards and then walks away will come back. We are expected to believe that the bus will stop where it promises to stop. That the treadmill will not let us walk ourselves to death because it decides to stop registering our steps.

If the world is going to work, there have to be large doses of faith invested in keeping it running. There needs to be a sort of cosmic "buddy system" by which we are protected from absolute chaos by holding on to some level of belief in "the other guy." In this kind of world, Aunts are ideal people to teach their Nieces and Nephews about faith. From the very start, it is evident that Aunts are people who are there for their Nieces and Nephews because they want to be, not just because they have to be. They are people with whom Nieces and Nephews can feel safe; be safe. They are people who make it just a bit easier for Nieces and Nephews to believe that when they act on faith, there's a good chance they won't be disappointed.

Things an Aunt Never Wants to Hear

(from Her Nieces/Nephews and Vice Versa)

*T*he Niece/Nephew Speaks . . .

- "I'm moving to *your town* next month, but I haven't been able to find an apartment, so I was wondering . . . ?"
- "The worst thing's just happened . . . now, you can't tell Mom and Dad . . . but . . . "
- "Is the movie almost over? . . . I feel sick!"
- "I told Mom and Dad I like coming to your house because you don't have all kinds of rules, like they do."
- "Are you a lot older than my Mom?"
- "I'm sure you wouldn't disapprove of Kimberley (. . . or Keith . . . or . . .)."
- "Aunt Sue, how come Timmy didn't get off the bus with us?"

The Aunt Speaks . . .

- "Vegetables most certainly are a part of life in this house!"
- "Don't worry, Honey. Things won't change a bit while your Parents are away . . . they've left me notes on your schedule, doctor's appointments, homework, and even a list of suggested menus."
- "Well, *I* don't approve."
- "I always watch CNN."
- "We can go there together!"
- "It's my favorite restaurant—The Virtuous Vegetarian."
- "Your Uncle and I asked the Browns to bring their Niece Grace; we're sure you two will have a lot in common."

"Part-Time Children"

*I*n case you're afraid that some manic "human resources" expert has infiltrated this book, dictating that not even children are immune from the 1990s' passion for "downsizing," breathe a sigh of relief. The idea came, instead, from a television producer who has used her gift for understanding the times to create segments for *Good Morning America*, *Oprah*, and MSNBC. When she was presented with the idea of a book about Aunts, Rita Barry's instant, word-association response was this exact phrase, "Oh, right, part-time children."

That would have been an interesting insight coming from anyone. But coming from someone whose profession depends on recognizing and presenting stories that reflect millions of viewers' real way of seeing things, it's more than just interesting. It is an invitation to explore the idea, to think it through, to follow it to wherever it leads. And so the thoughts began. And this is where they led.

The "Getting" and the "Going"

Since the bond that ties an Aunt to her Nieces and Nephews is definitely a forever thing, what is it that qualifies her and them as "part-time"? There's no cosmic alarm that rings— say, at age twelve—to tell either of you to shake hands, separate, and say, "Well, it was nice to know you." Nor is it a matter of an Aunt's lining them up someday to say that she regrets she can no longer keep them on her health insurance policy. That she will, with regret, have to ask them to pay by the day for vacation time spent with her.

If not these things, then, what does the "part-time" designation imply? Here's a possibility. It's a matter of "getting" and of "going."

The Aunt's "getting" of her Nieces and Nephews appears to be a lot less time-consuming than either pregnancy or adoption. But look more closely. Consider that an Aunt's upfront investment of herself in the "getting" of Nieces and Nephews actually involves many more years than either. The difference is that the Aunt's has usually been made long before the Nephew or Niece is even remotely a spark in anyone's eye. The odd and amazing thing is that they come as gifts to the Aunt from other people in her life: Brothers, Sisters, friends. The Aunt's bond with her Nieces and Nephews comes to be, initially, because of a relationship that existed quite independently of them. They come to her as a sort of extravagant "fringe benefit" of a bond with someone else. So, the cost of getting them was, so to speak, paid in advance. If it caused discomfort, left scars, or required endless amounts of interviewing, negotiating, and legal counseling, these are usually well in the past by the time the new Niece or Nephew arrives. All right, point taken. If the getting of them is a criterion, they could qualify as "part-time" children.

The real difference, though, is the "going." The fact is that Aunts and Nieces and Nephews all get to go home from each other. When teething leads to Olympic-class fretting; when the Cheerios have been tossed off of the high chair tray and onto the floor for what seems like the 400th time; when answers to the question "Why?" are finally and ultimately exhausted; when the phrase "But he . . . but she . . . " is ricocheting off the family room walls faster than the bullets in a John Ford movie; when the bedroom door slams shut and a teenager has decreed that adults are obviously incapable of understanding life's human issues; when the prospective bride steadfastly refuses to appear at her own wedding if Mr. and Mrs. X are invited—at, or shortly after, these not-so-cherished moments, an Aunt has, at the very least, the prospect of leaving the scene and returning home. Or to put it another way, the Aunt can leave without being arrested for abandonment when the going gets tough, or the tough get to be two years old.

This very issue of an Aunt's ability to go home without losing her rating as a "good Aunt" could lead to certain strains in the relationship responsible for getting her the Nieces or Nephews in the first place. It is possible that an Aunt may hear a slight note of irony in a Mother's voice as she says to her mutinous troops, "Say goodbye to Aunt Sue, children; she's going home." She doesn't say, "Say goodbye to Auntie Benedict Arnold, children." Not out loud, anyway.

So, as you leave, just keep a few factoids in mind. The

average number of diapers "consumed" by an infant in an average week is somewhere over seventy-six. And you're not there for most of them. Infants are the single most dependent group of mammals in nature, and most of them require some kind of help nearly every hour of what was once known to your Sister/Brother/friend as his or her sleeping hours. And, most of the time in the aptly titled dead of the night, you are at a safe distance from the cries of that ultimately needy little mammal.

As you smilingly present the beautiful little batiste (needs ironing) outfits, try to think of the daily average of three changes of clothes that an infant requires. As you wave a welcome to the approaching carful of Nieces, Nephews, and the people who live with them, don't forget to reflect on the amount of time, patience, logistical genius, and sheer grit that it took to assemble all those inner and outer clothes, matched socks, and age-appropriate toys (for diversionary use during the trip to your dwelling). It's most likely that you didn't do all that. Remember the persons who did, and think of them with full-time gratitude for giving you your part-time children.

The Secrets of Part-Time Children

Who could disagree that there are certain things in life that are better left unsaid? A fair few of them relate to an Aunt's part-time children.

Never, but never, say, especially in the presence of one or more Parents or full-time caregivers of your Nieces and Nephews, any of the following.
- "No, they didn't cry after you left."
- "Of course not, he/she was a perfect angel."

- "Gosh, he/she seemed to love the spinach last week at my house."
- "Trouble getting them to go to bed? Why, whatever do you mean?"
- "I never heard him/her play that music so loudly at our house."
- "They're apparently the only children who ever spent three hours at FAO Schwarz and never asked for anything."
- "The moment I said they needed to get out of the pool, they just hopped out immediately."
- "I never knew a child who was so eager to do homework."
- "But, he told me he wasn't going to date Jane anymore."
- "Don't they ever ask to borrow the car?"
- "It's amazing how similar our taste is in movies. She seems to love any film I suggest renting."
- "Their teacher Mrs. Milgrim said she'd actually found them all up-to-date on their work after the week they spent with us."
- "No, I'm sure they wouldn't mind if you stayed another week. They seem to have forgotten that they were only going to be here for the weekend."
- "Their friends are just as polite and punctual as they are."
- "But, they told me they love having me baby-sit."
- "You really should try serving regular meals; they seem to respond so well to them."
- "Isn't it wonderful how disciplined they are about stopping the video games the moment you call!"
- "I'm so glad to hear he/she isn't intrigued with body piercing."

- "How could I object when he/she assured me that you approve of the puce hair?"
- "Get home late? Philip? Of course, you're joking."
- "No, I'm not tired. I took a little snooze on the way over. Chris is such a good driver that I never have a care when he's at the wheel."
- "No, we didn't have trouble finding a restaurant. Ashley suggested this amazing little steak house near campus. It was terrific, and a bargain at that."
- "There's a television set in the guest room, but he seemed to enjoy watching with us."
- "Isn't it marvelous how much he has saved for tuition from that after-school job?"
- "If Jimmy weren't so patient, I'd never have learned to program the VCR."
- "She obviously got all her Internet surfing out of her system before she started using our setup."
- "I can't imagine why you wouldn't love David; he seems so right for her."
- "I think it's sweet that they want a small, simple wedding."
- "Emma hinted that you two are helping them with the down payment on the house."
- "Gosh, they call *me* every week."

Just remember, part-time children have full-time Parents who once were, and (if you learn when *not* to speak) could remain forever, your full-time friends.

A

Program
Note

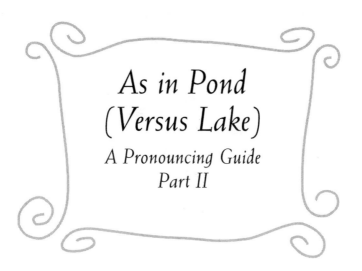

As in Pond (Versus Lake)
A Pronouncing Guide
Part II

So, let's say you've "tried on" the Aunt = Ȯnt pronunciation and it doesn't quite fit. Don't be concerned: there are lots more options where that one came from. For example, the "pond" approach.

The Aunt as in Pond (Versus Lake) Option

This pronunciation borrows the *o* the dictionary shows as an *a* with two dots above it (ä). Which quickly sends you looking to the key at the bottom of the page, where you find "ä—cot, cart" (which don't sound all that much alike to me and suggest that even the Merriam Webster folks don't seem to find this one easy to capture). Turning to the front of the dictionary, I find that this *o* as in ä is the one spoken by "most Americans" when they say, "Father." Maybe "cot, cart" would be better, after all.

In this case you call her (or are called) Aunt = Änt (and are on your own in predicting exactly how it will sound).

It appears that this pronunciation is mostly a matter of attitude. It's for people who may have a secret desire to sound like one of England's "royals," but don't admit it. Fans of this pronunciation probably enjoyed Fran Drescher as *The Nanny* but definitely don't want to *be* her.

Consequences

If you happen to have an Aunt Cot or Aunt Cart, this is definitely for you (even the dictionary people are on your side). If you don't, but still prefer the pronunciation, consider *pretending* to have both an Aunt Cot and an Aunt Cart (you can suggest they are from the long-lost branch of the family living in Auckland, whom you never see).

If you are about to become an Aunt for the first time and want very much to be called Aunt = Änt, you should be prepared to do some teaching/indoctrinating/brainwashing on behalf of the subtle pronunciation you've chosen. You could, for instance, begin talking a great deal about the absent but beloved Aunts = Änts Cot and Cart, thereby establishing the ground rules for how you want your title to be pronounced. Refer to her/their letters which have taught you so much about the charm of kangaroos, saying "Aunt = Änt Cot/Cart says there is nothing like a marsupial for a pet . . . etc." If you do a really good talking campaign, it should be crystal clear by the time the new Niece/Nephew arrives how it is that you want your title to be pronounced, which is necessary, because you haven't picked the easiest one. It's about as obvious as white-on-white printed fabric.

If you find you have to pronounce the title by itself, without a proper name attached, be prepared to be misunderstood or misjudged. People who live outside of the chic parts of London may conclude that you have a hidden commitment to speaking Oxonian English. It will become harder and harder to pass yourself off as "just plain folks."

Setting the Stage

The performance really starts coming together when the actors leave the rehearsal room and actually go on stage. They may even begin to look different. That certainly happens to the Aunt. She realizes that this stage has the power to transform a woman with a pacifier in her pocket and cookie crumbs in her car and show her for the serious performer she is. She finds new meaning in old lines (and songs). She realizes that where the part is played can be very important. It's starting to feel real. She realizes that having this role is changing her life.

Aunthood
Signs and Dead Giveaways

*T*hings change when you become an Aunt. There are signs that you will notice. And there are signs that no one can miss. Here are a mixed lot of some of those changes.

1. You carry a pacifier in your handbag.
2. You begin to cut the meat on your date's plate.
3. You say, "Now, what have we decided to order," when you sit down in a restaurant with your friends.
4. Discovery Zone, Gymboree, Little League, and soccer practice appear repeatedly in your date book.
5. You take off dangling earrings and all shiny jewelry before entering your Niece/Nephew's presence.
6. Your cleaning bills get noticeably higher.
7. Your car gets noticeably sandier/grassier/more scuffed, and filled with cookie crumbs.

8. Your car starts looking decidedly small to you.

9. Your car trunk contains: odd socks, toy trucks, books with several torn pages, and a mitten that belongs to no one.

10. Not only do you know what a sippy cup is, but you also can pull one off of your shelf in any primary color at a moment's notice.

11. You put out fresh linens when the phone rings (even before you answer it).

12. Your electronic organizer's "Birthdays" category is on overload.

13. You keep a full supply of birthday cards in your desk at work.

14. You show a startling knowledge of grade school curricula.

15. You have an opinion on the relative merits of breakfast cereals that come in packages the size of small human beings.

16. When applying the brakes, you instinctively put your right arm across the puzzled adult who happens to be occupying the right passenger seat in your car.

17. Your porcelain figurines are arranged, tin-soldier-style, on the top shelf of the bookcase.

18. You have six sets of keys for your small but centrally located apartment.

19. Your photo developing bills are higher than those for makeup, manicures, and hairstyling combined.

20. You're relieved to hear that the owner of the local frame shop, with whom you are on a first-name basis, just signed a new, ten-year lease.

21. You constantly run out of picture frames.

22. You begin to rate your neighbors on the basis of whether or not they have children the right age to play with visiting Nieces and Nephews.

23. Your video library now includes all the Disney classics.

24. Stuffed animals have permanently assumed prominent seating positions on your living room couches and queen-sized bed.

25. All the advice you've given your sibling about discipline, maintaining boundaries, and so on slides right out of your head the moment your two-year-old Niece or Nephew learns to pronounce some semblance of your name.

26. You firmly advise your sibling that you can spend two hours, and two hours only, baby-sitting on Sunday afternoon. Five hours later, when you and her child return, you find she is about to file a missing persons report and/or launch a kidnapping investigation.

Your Place or Mine?

Anyone who has studied military history knows that winning battles or losing them is more than a matter of geography. It wasn't just that Wellington was at Waterloo. It was a matter of being there at the right time, with the right number of people, with the right number of skills, with the right amount of food and provisions and uniforms and . . . It's beginning to sound like taking children to camp or to soccer practice, which is instructive, especially when it comes to the matter of Aunts and weekend baby-sitting, or even full-day visits.

D day worked because the Allies knew all the things that could go wrong and planned for them.

Aunts who plan to visit, or be visited by, their Nieces or Nephews could take a lesson from that bit of history.

The Aunt's Visit: On Their Turf

This may seem the easier route. But, don't be lulled into a false sense of confidence. Remember that while visiting Nieces and Nephews on their own turf spares you the challenge of finding storage space for the massive amounts of material required for the feeding and basic maintenance of preadult human beings, it also delivers certain special challenges. Here are some of the factors to consider.

- On their own turf, Nieces and Nephews know where the essentials are kept—and you don't. Clothes, food, video remote controls, pet food, soap, paper products, and extra diapers should be, but often are not, kept in logical places. Or more to the point, not in what *you* consider the logical places. All this is even more complicated in the periods before the Nieces/Nephews you are visiting have learned to: (a) speak and/or (b) reason. There you are, having run the water into the washing machine. The only clothes and socks that fit have been immersed. Your Nephew stands before you, smiling. A charming smile, you always believed. But, now the smile loses some of its charm because, he being preverbal, that smile is all he can give you, and what you really need is the secret of where the detergent is kept.

- On their own turf, Nieces and Nephews know all or most of the people who will show up at the door over the course of an average weekend. You don't. So, when the doorbell rings and a reasonably unthreatening person stands waiting for you to answer, you have no real way of establishing whether this is an ax murderer with the happy faculty of looking innocent or is, in fact, the neighbor who is coming to volunteer to drive in the car pool.

Even when your Nieces and Nephews have developed a reasonably serviceable vocabulary and have mastered the art of reasoning, that's no guarantee they will be able to tell you what you really want to know about the persons who appear, unannounced, at the door or call, unexpectedly, on the phone. So, you are reduced to repeating, more times than most people want to hear, "I really don't know . . . I'm only the Aunt. Just visiting for the weekend."

- On their own turf, the members of the household know about some of the ecological challenges the departing parents have not thought to mention. Take this real case report from an honorary Aunt. She was in charge. The children were both kind and observant. They were willing to grit their teeth and do what she suggested. She suggested that they go out to a certain part of the yard to play. They looked wary. They went. The bees came —as the regulars to the yard probably knew they would. The honorary Aunt leapt the distance from house to yard in one step, rescued the children in the nick of time, but felt like the role model for Snow White's Wicked Stepmother. The moral of that story is that, when you are visiting, and the members of the household look mildly horrified as you send the dog out for the night, it's reasonable to suspect that he's used to sleeping indoors. And don't be surprised if he shows up in your bed.

The Aunt's Visit: On Her Turf

- Unless the Aunt has children of exactly the same age as her Nieces and Nephews, there are likely to be adaptations that need to be made before her home is really ready to accommodate them. The term *babyproofing* sounds so quick and automatic. Just a few minor adjustments and, *voilà*, there you have it. It is only when a childless Aunt, or one whose own children have grown up, prepares for the visit of her infant Niece/Nephew that she realizes how many fragile/vulnerable/breakable objects and accessories she has in her life. And how many electrical outlets. And how expensive those little things are that you use to cover all these outlets. It is only when this otherwise benign, small person arrives and begins exploring that she realizes how few storage surfaces she has that are at least five feet above ground level. It may, in fact, be a good idea for some enterprising retailers like Ikea or Crate and Barrel to develop a line of collapsible, easy-to-install "hiding places" for Aunts to use when they are being visited by toddling Nieces or Nephews. It would be a simple, not unsightly, sturdy (yes, say it like it is, indestructible) set of shelves that can somehow be suspended from the ceiling, and that can accommodate all breakable objects that cannot be placed in storage pieces with closable/lockable doors.

- Even on her own turf, the Aunt being visited by her Nieces/Nephews should expect for her neighborhood to take on a totally foreign appearance. The things/places that have become familiar to her are very unlikely to be the things/places she really needs during their visit. What good is it to know where the gym is when what you really need is Gymboree or Discovery Zone? What use is the neighborhood's cute little French bistro when what you really need is King Cone or Burger King? What use is the little art film cinema when you need all the millimeters and Dolby degrees possible?

- Even on her own turf, the Aunt being visited by her Nieces/Nephews can expect her friends and neighbors to seem less desirable than ever in the past. What use is that wise, compassionate friend who has no household members under the age of twenty-one?

- An urban Aunt should be prepared to deal with culture shock when being visited by her suburban or rural Nieces/Nephews, whatever their age. If she inhabits a typically cramped big-city apartment, she needs to rehearse her answer when her visitors ask, "Where's the rest?" They mean rooms. The good news is that at a certain age, they will be willing to trade the room for the sensation of being in a tree house without the tree. Milk that one for all it's worth. It doesn't last long, and as the Nieces and Nephews get taller and larger, the small apartment gets to look proportionally smaller until it becomes a scene from *Gulliver's Travels*. And remember, there's a vice-versa scenario when the urban Nieces and Nephews visit "the country." Unless it's really deep country and they are closet outdoor types, the rural Aunt can expect to live through a period of crowd withdrawal and pointed comments about those irritating crickets at night and roosters at dawn.

In other words, it's no easier answering the question "Your place or mine?" posed by Nieces and Nephews than it is to answer it in the more usual social context.

I know of one family whose members decided to keep and co-own a huge, rambling Victorian house in the country that had belonged to an earlier generation of their family. When they are together there, everyone is, happily, on his or her own turf. They seem to have the only really good answer to the question. And the answer is: "*Our* place."

But, until the gods of mortgages and real estate smile upon them, Aunts, Nieces, and Nephews should remember the lessons of Waterloo and remind themselves that geography is not destiny. As long as each knows what to expect, and prepares for it, the answer to that question, "Your place or mine?" is, "Either would be great, as long as you'll be there."

"The First Time Ever I Saw Your Face"

Whoever had the idea of recording Beatles melodies as lullabies was inspired.

Most really good songs have a second life. And that new and often rich life comes about when a familiar melody or set of lyrics is connected in the listener's mind with a new person or situation. By such a variety of circumstances, certain songs become connected in an Aunt's mind with her Niece or Nephew. The songs may not have been written for that reason or have any apparent connection with children in general, or with that child in particular, but somehow a special link develops. And forever after, that song speaks of that person. When you hear it, you could almost be tempted to mouth that classic line, "Listen, they're playing our song."

That is precisely what happened in a most amazing way with the beautiful Carly Simon song "You're the Love of My Life" in the film *This Is My Life*. Viewers and listeners were drawn to find a fresh interpretation of what seemed, on the face of it, to be a romantic love song as it became the background music to a Mother's looking at her children.

That connection became even more real, off the screen, when my Nephew Patrick and his wife, Tina, were awaiting the birth of their adopted son Liam. They mentioned more than once that they had found the song and its context very moving and had come to connect it with the child who would be coming into their lives. That particular song and that connection had gone out of everyone's minds with the emotion of going to the hospital to meet him and bring him back to their home. Then, as the car pulled out of the hospital driveway, "You're the Love of My Life" began to play on the car radio, and its words and the added dimension they now had became so remarkably real and so moving. It will always, in my mind, be Liam's special song.

For Kevin, it will be the George Winston music used as the background of Meryl Streep's wonderful recorded reading of The Velveteen Rabbit. I was playing the Wyndham Hill CD one day when Kevin, not yet six, walked into the apartment and said, "Listen, The Velveteen Rabbit," making the music, forever, his song.

Some truly amazing songs have been written for children and about them. By Stevie Wonder for example, serenading the child he could not see in the traditional sense but whom he saw deeply and clearly enough to give all the rest of us a new reason to love "Isn't She Lovely?" Eric Clapton, Elton John . . . the names and the reasons for singing of children are so many and so creative.

But, for those who cannot write their own songs, there are ones that they can adopt to send a message to their Nieces and Nephews.

How better to tell them of the special place they hold in your life than to do it with the Beatles classic "In My Life."

And at one of the many moments when the Aunt's role is to encourage and lend support as a Nephew or Niece wrestles with the decisions that are part of growing up, there are enormous talents out there to help her give words and music to that encouragement. None better than the brilliant singer-songwriter-musician—bard, Judy Collins. Her compositions "My Father" and "Secret Gardens" could be classics in any family. And her "Trust Your Heart" is one of the best ways I know of introducing a dialogue with a Niece or Nephew on the subject of confidence. Developing it. Being convinced you have a right to it. Learning to edit out the instincts that are only self-serving and to bank on the ones that are humane.

Kate Winn of RCA says she will always have a "music connection" with the birth of her first Niece. She had been listening to and loving Marvin Gaye's "Mercy Me" in the months while Katie Barnes was expected. The call came at 5 A.M. one day, to say that she had arrived. Needless to say, the new Aunt had some trouble getting back to sleep, and when she turned on her radio, there was that song. Only now when she listened to the words about how we are endangering our planet's ecology, it suddenly had a whole new meaning, because now she was thinking about it as a world her generation would be handing on to the new generation represented by her new Niece.

Digging in a secondhand record store becomes worth all the effort and all the dust when you unearth a copy of an album of songs for children, sung by Danny Kaye and written by Milton Schafer. "Colored Kisses" is one of the

loveliest ways imaginable of telling children that the many
people who love them will each do so in a distinctive way.

Roberta Flack made Ewan MacColl's song her own when
she recorded "The First Time Ever I Saw Your Face." So,
maybe neither of them would mind that an Aunt adopt the
song to accompany the annual birthday ritual. You will
quickly notice that one of the stories children love most is
the one they ask their Parents to recount when they say,
"Tell me about when I was born." And as with all of childhood's most treasured stories, they want to hear it again
and again. Even before they've developed a taste for the
music of grown-ups, they will know instinctively, when you
use these words and this music to accompany your retelling
of the story, that it is because the first time you saw each
of their faces was such a uniquely important event. And perhaps the music will help them understand just how important their first appearance was. So, while Parents repeat the
narrative one way, an Aunt can call on some of the artists
she enjoys to find another way of telling Nieces and
Nephews what she remembers of the day they were born.

Who knows what Dan Hill had in mind when he wrote
"Sometimes When We Touch"? Or what their images were
as Cleo Laine and James Galway made their superb recording of it. But an Aunt can find a new vein of meaning when
she hears that song and remembers the impact of experi-
encing the bond that makes a Niece or Nephew a permanent, miraculous part of her life. She may have to wait until
they have Nieces and Nephews of their own before they
will understand.

On the other hand, it is very clear what Ireland's most
popular recording artist had in mine when he wrote the
song "Scorn Not His Simplicity." Phil Coulter was passing

from denial to acceptance and affirmation of his child, who had been born with Down's syndrome. It is a song that an Aunt can use if she is called on to make that same, demanding passage.

It is probably easier to build bridges between Aunts and their Nieces and Nephews than it is to bring together her music and theirs. But when they know that some of her music is music in which she finds some images of them, they may be intrigued enough to listen with new ears.

Listen to the words of Kenny Loggins's "For the First Time." It's a love song, right? Now listen as an Aunt who sees her Niece or Nephew "for the first time," and see what happens to the song. Or revisit Van Morrison's "Have I Told You Lately," and listen with an Aunt's ears. It can be quite a revelation. Here's one that can be listened to with new ears by both Aunts and their Nieces and Nephews: Harold Melvin and the Blue Notes singing his "If You Don't Know Me by Now."

Sometimes it may be from the point of view of "history" that an Aunt can say, "They're playing our song," reminding a Niece or Nephew that "This song was number one the year you were born."

Other times it can be when either of them has feelings that are challenging to express. "This song reminds me of you because . . . (and here they fill in the experiences that are drawn from both of their lives)." In either case, an Aunt and her Niece or Nephew will be realizing the power of songs' "second lives." There's a song that's perfect for just such a moment. It's the Rodgers and Hammerstein classic from *The King and I*, and it's called—of course: "Getting to Know You." A very pleasant task, and one in which music can play a very positive role.

The Props

The props can't make a performance. But they can ruin it, if the actor doesn't learn how to handle them and make them work. That is a vital thing for the Aunt to realize. And it's not just the props she has on stage that she must master. She can sometimes be betrayed by the contents of her garage or have her performance enhanced by the contents of her bookshelves. Unless the Aunt gives her props their due, she runs the risk of having her performance undone by a collapsible stroller.

A Table
of
Contents

This is not a "lost chapter," set down by a printer's error in the wrong place in the book. It is an attempt to deal with the fact that an Aunt's refrigerator, her garage, her bookshelves can often say as much about her as what she says or does. Knowing that, the Aunt can be forgiven for fantasizing a bit about what she'd *like* her garage to say about her, what she'd *like* her refrigerator and her bookshelves to say to her Nieces/Nephews, and what she is determined to have her bookshelves say.

It's amazing how much each of these says about Aunts as they are, as they might like to be, and as their Nieces and Nephews would probably like them to be.

Listen for yourself.

Contents: Aunt's Garage

Height of Fantasy Version

1. Maserati, red
2. Ten-speed bicycle
3. Skis
4. Scuba gear
5. Lawn chair, suitable for sunning
6. Treadmill/heavily used/no reading rack
7. Six cans tennis balls
8. Golf bag carrier/first-class airline tags still in place
9. Helmet suitable for use on Harley Davidson
10. Harley Davidson

Contents: Aunt's Garage

Midway Between Fantasy and Reality Version

1. Mercedes Benz sports car, dark blue
2. Ten-speed bicycle
3. Skis (cross-country)
4. Swim goggles
5. Discarded sun lamp
6. Collapsible treadmill (still in original packing carton)
7. Three tennis balls
8. Portable putting trainer (with lightly used original packaging)
9. Straw hat suitable for gardening
10. Motorized scooter

Contents: Aunt's Garage
Actual

1. 1989 Ford Tempo (40,000 miles on odometer)
2. Lightly used stationary bike
3. Snow boots
4. Swim cap, nose plug, ear plugs, SPF 30 lotion
5. Picnic table with partially collapsed umbrella
6. Ab trainer (still in original packing carton)
7. Sand buckets, miniature shovels, three unmatched children's socks
8. Badminton set (in slightly dusty, crumpled original packaging)
9. Snow shovel/rake
10. Jump rope

Contents of Aunt's Refrigerator/Cupboard Revealing the Presence of Niece/Nephew, Aged Zero–Six

1. Apple juice, industrial size
2. Apple juice, individual containers
3. Cheerios, massive size
4. Milk/1–2 percent fat maximum
5. Ovaltine/Nestlé's Quik/Hershey's Syrup
6. Animal crackers
7. Emergency Gummi Bears (hidden behind brussels sprouts)
8. Children's Tylenol
9. Chewable vitamins (preferably bright colors, recognizable shapes)
10. Teething ring (freezer)

Contents of Aunt's Refrigerator/Cupboard Revealing the Presence of Niece/Nephew, Aged Seven–Twelve

1. Juice, anything *but* apple, mammoth size
2. Jelly, to go with peanut butter, both mammoth size
3. Ketchup, industrial pump version
4. Bread, restaurant-size loaves
5. Sliced chicken, turkey, bologna, almost anything edible
6. Instant herbal iced tea mix, a size Aunt believes will last for six months but that actually lasts 2.4 visits
7. Apples, by the treeful
8. S'mores ingredients (for nostalgia purposes)
9. Popsicles (classic and culturally updated versions in shape of Power Rangers, Barney, Bananas in Pajamas, Simba, Jasmine, et al.)
10. Pizza, exclude anchovy topping (freezer)

Contents of Aunt's Refrigerator/Cupboard Revealing the Presence of Niece/Nephew, Adult

1. Raw bran
2. Two salsas: one mild, one spicy
3. V-8, large glass container
4. Brita filter, large size
5. Finn Crisps
6. Raw vegetables, cut to bite size
7. Condiments, all opened, none fully consumed
8. Yogurt, pint size, plain, fat-free
9. Tofu-based cheese substitute
10. Extra bottle nail polish in favorite, hard-to-find color

The Aunt's Bookshelves

Your five-year-old nephew sits rapt, as you read to him, until he suddenly develops a puzzled look and says, "But where are the pictures? I don't see any pictures. How do we know what the children in the story look like?"

When that happens, let it sound an alarm in your mind.

Tell him that the pictures of the children and where they live and what they see are there, in his imagination. And then, make a resolution to include a book in every gift to him—and to all the children in your life.

Depending on when she was born, and when they were, Nieces/Nephews may think it quaint for their Aunt to have bookshelves—actually filled with books. As fund-raising letters written on behalf of libraries remind us, the book may become an endangered species in a world dominated by CD-ROMs. So, it's important for Aunts to remember that the book has been, is, and probably should always be one of her "signs of office," equivalent to a police officer's badge, a firefighter's hat, or a doctor's stethoscope.

The sound of an Aunt reading to her Nieces/Nephews is the sound of a woman knitting herself into the fabric of their lives. And even, or perhaps especially, if her Nieces/Nephews are born and bred nerdlettes immersed in the age of computers, she should do all that she can to ensure that they grow up able to recognize a book and the magic it can create.

So, the ideal contents of an Aunt's Niece/Nephew-friendly bookshelves can be described in one word, *"everything"* with the exception of what is second-rate. The classics, humor, poetry, drama, glorious coffee-table books, and reference works of every kind. Fiction and nonfiction; new books and used ones; books in every language she and her Nieces and Nephews know or aspire to know. Books about their ethnic roots. Books of music. Books signed by authors and books bought at flea markets. Books with copious notes in the margins.

Books about people the Aunt wants her Nieces/Nephews to meet. And places she wants them to see. And principles she wants them to value. And ideas she wants them to wrestle with. Books that are reminders of what it was like when illustrators became famous: Arthur Rackham and N. C. Wyeth, Beatrix Potter and Shel Silverstein. She needn't fret if her electronics are not up-to-date. She should lament only if her bookshelves are bare. Or if her Nephews and Nieces have not heard many of the books it contains, read to them in her voice.

Gearing Up
for Aunthood

*I*t begins when someone who has not yet spent two full years on earth looks at you indulgently, takes pity on you and your obvious bewilderment, and shows you how to buckle and unbuckle his or her car seat.

Welcome to the "gear gap."

It's the equipment equivalent of the generation gap which separates childless Aunts not only from their young Nieces/ Nephews and their Parents but also from married-with-children Aunts who have résumés to prove that they have cracked the code of Aunt-resistant car seats, folding strollers, flip-top changing tables, and childproof aspirin caps.

Fortunately, children turn out to be a lot more compassionate than most adults and will often bail you out when it becomes clear that the umbrella-style collapsible stroller cannot, in fact, be folded wafer thin using the one hand that is not occupied with holding on to a little one, fishing for the bus token, and beating off the assault of the grand-motherly looking person whose sympathy with your plight seems to have deserted her.

Like golf and yachting, being an Aunt is a hobby that requires you to own and/or operate huge amounts of challenging and complicated equipment. It is wise to know that and to be on the lookout for certain of the most threatening elements of the "gear trap."

Advice to Aunts Concerning the "Gear Trap"

Strollers These supposedly benign, even helpful pieces of equipment are really designed to test the new Aunt's mental acumen, patience, humility, brute strength, cunning, and ability to withstand the temptation to use undeleted expletives. To meet these tests be aware of these points.

Collapsible as used to describe these vehicles does not refer to the stroller itself, but rather to the Aunt, who is likely to collapse before she figures out how to reduce said stroller to a size that permits it to fit through normal, domestic-sized doors; into the trunk of an automobile not purchased for use by groups the size of baseball teams or larger; or aboard any type of public transportation. Be aware that there are distinctly different forms of collapsibility, deceptively described in the sales and product enclosure literature with terms related to equipment you think you know how to operate. "Umbrella-style," for example, hints that the stroller can be whipped from fully assembled to easily totable as easily as one raises or lowers an umbrella. In your dreams! There are also inward-folding and outward-folding styles. The former is designed to snap shut on one or more of your outer garments as you try to reduce its unwieldy bulk; the latter requires that you have a width of arm spread and a degree of strength in your (fully extended) fingertips that would excite envy in The Hulk, himself. As for the front-to-back collapsers, they are apparently designed to be dropped from an upper-story window so that they can be collected, neatly compacted, by the time you and your Niece/Nephew have walked down the stairs and also reached ground level.

Double is a designation you are likely to be looking for and dealing with in this era of fertility drugs and rampant multiple birthing. Don't let your commitment to fair play and desire to avoid putting the twin Nieces/Nephews into situations where one must be "first" and the other "second" fool you into thinking there is a redeeming social value in a two-abreast stroller. While it ensures that both children get a first and unobstructed view of everything that falls in their path, it severely limits the places you can actually take them and the stroller in order to get even one unobstructed view. They're great in ballrooms and ballparks, but only if the former is otherwise empty and the latter can be reached via helicopter drop. So, opt for the single-file model and change the babies' positions to ensure that baby number two sees more than just the back of baby number one's head. And remember that revolving doors are completely out of bounds and that you need to stay three times farther away from the oncoming traffic when you cross the street by foot.

Braking systems on strollers are more complicated than those on the most eccentric Italian sports car. Locking and unlocking them and doing so for one, two, three, or four wheels at a time is no easy matter. Failure to do so at the right time and in the right order will leave you pushing the firmly fixed wheels over sidewalks (if you're lucky) or pea stones (if your worst nightmare comes to life) or pushing the hysterically laughing Niece/Nephew around in tight little circles—which he or she is kind enough to think you are doing on purpose.

Diapers   If you still remember the dear, long-gone days when the only varieties of these were clean and dirty, you are in for a seismic shock. So, if you belong to the school of thought that says, "I love my Niece/Nephew unconditionally, except for changing," then skip ahead to the next section. You can keep your consciousness unencumbered, at least until you, too, reproduce or adopt.

Cloth or disposable seems like a pretty straightforward option. But you would have to have the sophistication of a Ph.D. in ecological sciences and the obsessive/compulsive commitment to detail of an efficiency expert to weigh all the pros and cons of this seemingly simple choice. And besides, once you've made that choice, it's only the beginning.

Size is no simple matter of "about this long" (said with arms extended to the appropriate dimension). If you are asked to "pick up some Pampers on your way over," don't leave home, or the telephone, without determining the current weight in pounds of the small person in need of underpinnings. You need to know this within a range so exact that you'd think it was designed for measuring gold bullion or you risk dropping the baby through the oversized leg opening of a wrong-sized diaper.

Style issues include: newborn or not; decorated with pictures of Barney or Mickey Mouse, or not; for night or day wear; and with or without self-adhesive tabs which, if they are opened before the baby is changed, stick to the changing table and, if opened afterward, stick (resolutely) to you. Be warned that your Nephew/Niece's style preferences develop at a frighteningly early moment in his or her life and that long before the first phrase is spoken, he or she will not be fooled if you try to substitute a Barney diaper for a Mickey. And remember too that this is one of the oases of non-PC designations. There really is a difference between male and female diapers, and you ignore it at your own peril.

By the time Niece/Nephew reaches what used to be called "the age of reason" the gear gets easier, but the highly developed preferences and peer pressures are building up, and so, it's wise for an Aunt to know that if the Niece/Nephew asks for a Tommy Hilfiger jacket and gets one by L.A. Gear, your stock drops so far and fast that Wall Street would call it an unqualified crash.

When the Niece/Nephew is heading for college, the technical nuances of sound equipment, computer hard- and software, and all wheeled vehicles are more surely within his or her grasp than the Top 40 were to you at his or her age.

It's enough to say that sooner, rather than later, living in the world of Niece/Nephew gear gets to be as challenging as, well . . . as a *stroller*.

The Gear Gap Hall of Fame

A List of Equipment Designed to Strike Terror into the Heart of the Childless Aunt

1. The rear-facing car seat
2. The Snugli/front-facing/back-facing/spoon-style/front wrapping/back-looping
3. The high chair/sliding-locking-tray style
4. The collapsible crib
5. The "potty" chair
6. The crib side extender
7. Nintendo 64
8. The skateboard
9. The dirt bike
10. The vehicle (as distinct from the car)

Playing the Part

*O*ne of the best things that can be said of any performance is that it was convincing. To pull off the role of the Aunt it's important to know that certain nuances of performance are the acid test for whether it is really convincing: the quality of the welcome, for example, and competence at the "Hug Test." The actress playing this role must never underestimate the importance of encouraging fantasy, and of being a good translator, a crack poker player, and a genius at transferring technology. The role of the Aunt is a challenging one and requires some very special skills if it's to be played convincingly.

Words of Welcome

*A*ssuming that you learn to speak before they do (one of a handful of statistically safe assumptions) your first gift to your new Niece or Nephew should be words of welcome. For a while, at least, the turf is yours and your fellow adults', and the newcomer status is theirs. So, be sure to say welcome. In words. Remember that it wasn't easy for them to get here. That it took some work. And that it probably seemed much easier where they were.

So, even if you feel a bit silly, be sure to say to this new person in your life, the very first time you meet, "You are so very welcome. We are all so glad that you came. We'll try to do everything we can to make sure that you feel at home."

I learned this habit several years ago when viewing an absolutely amazing interview on *Good Morning America*. The host was talking to a couple whose children were off-the-charts brilliant and trying to get at what it was that made them so remarkably intelligent. Instead of some rarified answer about teaching them calculus in the cradle, the Mother said quite simply, "Well, we have always tried to make them feel welcome." She encouraged saying welcome in words. It is advice I have taken to heart ever since. And none of the real and honorary Nieces and Nephews who have heard these words has disagreed.

When your Nieces and Nephews learn to speak, and even before, when they can use body language ranging from smiles to hugs to running leaps into your arms, they will often return the favor.

This speaking of welcome may not make either of you more intelligent than you were before, but it's sure to make you more human. Which may be what having Aunts/Nieces/Nephews is all about, anyway.

The Hug Test

Shopping is one of the activities that "come with the territory" of Aunthood. While all the things said about the spiritual qualities of your relationship with your Nieces and Nephews are true, it's wise to remember that the tokens of that special bond will, very likely, come from places other than the heart. Retail stores, for one. Banks and brokerages for another. Shortly after the birth announcement you are likely to hear a small, interior voice saying, "Go forth and shop." In that situation you just might appreciate some . . .

. . . General Advice for Aunts

- Shopping for your Nieces and Nephews begins and ends with the "hug test."

When they are tiny, remember that you want to find something they will want to hug. As they age, and you do too, remember that you want to find something that will make them want, spontaneously, to hug you.

So, What Is the Hug Test and How Does It Work?

When Shopping for an Infant Niece or Nephew

Shop with the new baby in mind. Not its parents. Stuffed animals and soft dolls will mean a great deal more to your new Niece or Nephew than the traditional silver cup or picture frame. Give yourself a little instant gratification. Find something that will be part of your new Niece's or Nephew's childhood memories. (I still remember the downy soft, yellow creature that was named "Swoose" because it looked like a combination of a swan and a goose. And the curly-coated black lamb whose peach-colored bow I loved to tatters long before my black sheep reached the same state.)

When in a store, leave your pride and self-consciousness at the door. Make sure to hug each potential selection with all the charming intensity your Niece or Nephew will bring to that work. I have uncovered many potential dangers from an offending, sharp-edged internal music box; scratchy whisker or antenna; and all-too swallowable glass eye by conducting the hug test while on the shopping floor.

The hug test, conducted in public, turns out also to be a good way to meet like-minded adults. Anyone who looks askance at you as you hug the various candidate toys is, you can be sure, someone you don't really care to meet. If, on the other hand, you meet eyes and smile over the teddy bears you are both hugging quite unselfconsciously, this may be someone you would like to know.

Retail environments that for any reason make it impossible to have hugging privileges with the candidate toys are ones you don't want to give business. Make sure to look for ones that seem to understand children, not just profit-and-loss statements.

Some For Instances

- I feel sure that a young man I once met at FAO Schwarz is now at least a director of that venerable toy store. He saw me hugging a succession of bears and said, "It's really important to find out which one is yours." If he isn't an officer of the corporation, they should find him and make him one instantly.

- Names can tell you a lot about the place you pick to shop for small Nieces and Nephews. I have a Niece who chose the name "The North Pole" for a store she opened. That kind of healthy respect for magic is something you want to keep alive in a world of fill-in-the-blanks predictability. Some other places I knew I'd want to shop were named: "Eeyore" and "Penny Whistle Toys," and "Uncle Futz" and "Promises Fulfilled." Shakespeare may have been right about the unimportance of Romeo's and Juliet's family names, but when it comes to hug-tested shopping, names can speak volumes.

When Shopping for an Older Niece or Nephew

Watch for the signs that your Niece's or Nephew's uniqueness is under attack. And use your gift shopping as a way of defending it. Be forewarned: you're going to be walking a tightrope! On one side is the newly socialized child who has gone out into the wider world of play groups and day care centers and schools; found that there are all those things that "everybody" has; and begun pleading to get them too. So, you can either shop for the Great American Clone or stretch your imagination and theirs by searching for and finding things that are special without being eccentric. Take it that no child of four to ten wants to be eccentric or to have an Aunt who is. (Being *wildly* eccentric is another matter—that is usually so far *out* as to be *in*, but that's another discussion altogether.)

At this age, the hug test involves the Niece's or Nephew's reaction to a gift: a hug that says, "You get it!" But, be careful. You don't want to "get it" to the point at which your gifts look as if they could have come from Aunt Central where a special impersonal shopper selects generic gifts famous for being just like the dreaded "everyone's." The "it" you want to "get" is the one that's on your adult agenda. Use the experience you were given before that Niece or Nephew arrived on the scene to figure out how to give a gift that includes growth. Use the shirt with the "23" that's turning every child in sight into a Michael Jordan wannabe to wrap a game that teaches about gravity, and then talk to the child about the fact that what makes that Chicago basketball player so amazing is his ability to defy it.

Remember that "Not clothes" is the expressed or unexpressed preference of nearly every Nephew—until he reaches prepuberty, a condition heralded by an almost slavish adherence to a strict uniform code which apparently is communicated directly from on high by a power unrelated to family or society. And even when he lusts for whatever is the preteen "uniform" of the hour, remember that he'd probably rather shop for it himself. Why else did God make gift certificates?

Note that dolls are either for looking at from a distance or for cherishing and generally killing with kindness at very close range. Rarely are they both. If you insist upon buying the "at a distance" variety don't be surprised to find that it is either treated as if it were a rag doll or ignored. And when it is treated like a rag doll, and you find that you are distressed, reread a book called *The Velveteen Rabbit* and get over it.

When Shopping for an Adult Niece or Nephew

An automobile (although I hear they have been made extinct by "vehicles" of the "R"—as in recreational—or "AT"—as in all-terrain—variety) is always a good bet. So is assumption of the remaining portion of his or her student loan, an apartment, and a trust fund. So much for fantasy. Now, on to pesky, limiting reality.

If your Nieces/Nephews now have children of their own, a book of coupons entitling the holder to a day/night/weekend or week of baby-sitting is a sure winner.

The older they become, the more fascinating their own childhoods become to them. Try keeping a box of mementos of each Niece or Nephew, and when they have grown old enough to appreciate these, put them together into a book or videotape as "An Aunt's-Eye View of David (or Emma)."

And Remember to Remember This in All Cases

The real gift is that new person in your life. Let that assurance motivate everything else, and you'll always be on solid ground as a truly gifted Aunt.

Places to Avoid When Shopping for Small Nieces/Nephews

Little Boys/Girls Should Be Seen . . .
Stiff Upper Lips R Us
Touch-Me-Not Toys
Electronic Wonderland
Modem Madness
Facts Are Fun
If You're Very Good
Nanny's
Hush and Be Good
Ask Me No Questions
Curiosity Killed the Cat

Places You'd Like to Find When Shopping for Small Nieces/Nephews

Rainy Day Magic
Learning Fun
Aunt Cuddly's
Best Friends
Experiments in Wonder
Take a Guess
Laughter Incorporated
Ever Wonder How?
Child Friendly
Come On In!
You're Welcome
More Fun Than a Barrel

The
Mary Poppins
Factor

Whimsy is to the Aunt's bond with Nieces and Nephews what oxygen is to diving. It keeps you going longer and gets you deeper than almost anything else. Aunts should consider taking a leaf, or two or three from *Mary Poppins*.

Being an Aunt is serious business, but an Aunt should be living proof of the fact that you don't have to be stuffy to get things done. Think of it as the "Mary Poppins Factor." Was there ever a more no-nonsense nanny? Or one that made getting on with life show up more clearly for what it is: being grown up enough to act like children?

Even before Julie Andrews, I knew that Mary Poppins was a woman to reckon with. Besides limiting herself to carry-on baggage only and still being able to bring along her four-poster bed and a lamp, this was obviously someone who knew how to live. She knew when to put her foot down and, especially, where to put it down: on the firm ground of life lived with a sense of humor and a sense of whimsy. Here's how an Aunt can do the same.

An Aunt's "To Do" List: Poppins Factor Version

- *Help your Niece/Nephew be brave in the choice of friends.* A chimney sweep. A Mr. Fixit who fixed everything but broken hearts. A pigeon fancier. A sidewalk artist. Unlikely choices for a lady who wore very conservative clothes and insisted on having rooms kept in perfect order. But these were the people Mary took for exactly who they were, people a lot like herself: people with special gifts who knew how to have fun and how to be kind—just different enough themselves to ensure that they wouldn't be hidebound in what they expected of their friends. This isn't a bad agenda for Aunts and for the Nieces and Nephews who need all the adult "case histories" they can find to illustrate that growing up does not mean selling out.

- *Help them get to the top without taking themselves too seriously.* Upward mobility never looked so attainable as when Mary Poppins and her young charges laughed themselves and the tea table to the ceiling of her Uncle Albert's. For contemporary children who have to compete from day one— for everything from places in play school through college courses and hard-to-find jobs—having an Aunt to act as an ally and whose home is part decompression chamber can provide an important safety valve. Lavish them with laughter. Not the kind that shows up in the Nebbish cartoon captioned "If you're still smiling, you obviously don't understand the problem." Nor Alfred E. Newman's *Mad* magazine inanity. Consider yourself a successful Aunt if you create an environment in which it is safe to laugh, even when you know the odds.

- *Help them recognize starting points.* Walking into landscapes drawn on a sidewalk, in chalk, could probably be anyone's idea of a great starting point. It would be fantastic. Literally. The art of the Aunt is to help your Niece/Nephew develop enough perspective to recognize even the most seemingly straightforward moments of life as valid starting points: for example, a test failure that helps move them into a field of study they enjoy more and so will be better at. It's amazing what a person can hear when a good sounding board is available. An Aunt who can listen is likely to encourage a Niece or Nephew to know how to listen to her or his own best instincts.

- *Help them recognize that a "spoonful of sugar" is no longer politically correct—for a good reason!* Whimsy is one thing. Foolishness is another. What you're about as an Aunt is helping Nieces/Nephews not to be *tyrannized* by reality. That doesn't include breaking with it entirely.

Searching for Bun
The Aunt as Translator

*Y*ou're alone with your Nephew and trying to get him and yourself out of the house. He is distraught. He can't go without "bun." So, you search the bread box, the bread drawer, the refrigerator, the freezer for the elusive roll. You try to entice him with every form of bread you can lay your hands on. But, all he can say is, "No, *bun*." And now with mounting sadness, "Bun!"

Finally, as you move to the cupboards and scour them for a cookie or biscuit that might fill the bill, he emerges with a scrap of once-blue textile clutched to his tear-stained face and says, triumphantly, "See, Bun!"

Bun had been a pillow cover once, blue gingham with a brown yarn rabbit decorating its surface. Now it is a symbol of the fact that every family has a secret language. And none of them has a United Nations–style system of simultaneous translation so that the satellite members of the family are supplied with a running interpretation of what is meant, versus what is said, when family members speak to each other.

So, being an Aunt is often being a translator. Knowing that when your Niece/Nephew asks for Happy, he or she is not asking to see the video of *Snow White*, but rather wants to see his or her maternal Grandmother. Sometimes this need for a translator is just amusing, or charming. It makes for good stories.

But, there are other times when the private language barrier has more practical implications. For example, various words for determining the necessity and/or urgency for using the sanitary facilities. The words for this set of activities can sometimes make Sanskrit look simple by comparison. Before consenting to be left alone for longer than one hour with an ambulatory Niece/Nephew, make certain to get a full and exhaustive list of all the words you need to listen for with a special urgency.

Absent that reassuring, earphoned translator, learn to look at your Niece/Nephew and read the visual cues. Because "Gaga" means one thing to you, don't assume it means the same to a three-year-old.

Become a good detective. Say things like, "Let's look for a picture of 'Gaga,'" or "Where does 'Gaga' stay?"

Be prepared for surprises. Consider this list of names for Grandfathers, for example. As the saying goes, "Who knew?"

Bumpy
Porgie
Doc
Poppa

Or for Grandmothers:

Happy
Gramby
Poops
Taloo

So, when you hear an unfamiliar name, just remember it could be the real carpenter, or an imaginary friend, or a very important stuffed animal. Nothing should surprise the well-prepared Aunt. If, for example, you are asked to move over to make room so that someone you don't see can sit down, don't argue; just move over. It could be that the charming, unattached bachelor neighbor is approaching and your Niece/Nephew has seen him first. Or it could be someone that lives only in the imagination of your Niece/Nephew. It's all part of being a member of a family that has its own, secret language.

The Aunt as Poker Player

ow important is it that an Aunt really know what she's doing?

Or what her Nieces/Nephews are doing?

If she is operating a vehicle in which her Nieces/Nephews are passengers, it's obviously vital that she know exactly what she's about. But, sometimes, it's more a matter of reassurance than reality.

It takes more than a little time and a lot of testing for the Aunt and her Nieces/Nephews to take each other's measure and develop their own rules for living.

At first, an Aunt assumes that her Nieces and Nephews need her to know "everything," to be a monument to certainty. Then, one day, and hope that it comes sooner rather than later, the Aunt is called upon to know an answer or a solution and hasn't a clue.

And then—and this is the really great moment—she realizes that they know, and know that she knows they know, that she really doesn't have a clue.

That moment can be the beginning of a really great relationship. When an Aunt who came into her Nieces' and Nephews' lives because of someone else's decisions emerges as somebody they really want to have in their lives, on their own terms, then a happy accident becomes a much happier conspiracy of freedoms. Without saying so, and even without entirely understanding what is happening, an Aunt and her Nieces and Nephews reach a silent understanding that what they need from her is more than certainty. It is honesty, with a large side order of humor. It is conversion from an authority figure into a figure of authentic authority. From the Nieces' and Nephews' point of view, it means that their Aunt has become more than one of an interchangeable set of adults who administer the instructions attached by a magnet to the refrigerator door.

The issue itself is not so important. It could be disarming the alarm system, or operating the microwave, or deciding the after-date curfew. The important thing is that an Aunt and her Nieces and Nephews learn that they can work things out together.

It's the moment when the Aunt who has kept up the poker player's facade of certainty sees and understands that she is free to be a little—or a lot—less than certain. The bargain is sealed with a smile that grows into a laugh, and a lifelong friendship is born.

Transfer of Technology, or, Keeping It in the Family

There's a wonderful nonprofit organization called ORBIS which operates the world's only airborne teaching eye hospital and takes volunteer doctors around the world to fight preventable blindness. It may be that the best thing they do is not just the miraculous, sight-restoring surgeries, but what they call "transfer of technology." That means teaching host-country doctors how to keep working the magic after the ORBIS plane leaves. In that way, in particular, ORBIS has a lesson to teach to Aunts.

Now, anyone who doesn't see the connection between Aunthood and nonprofit organizations obviously hasn't been an Aunt for long! It quickly becomes evident that whatever else Aunthood is, it is very unlikely ever to become a profit-making activity. The nonprofit connection is a natural. So, having accepted that fact, let's look at how "transfer of technology" applies to Aunts.

Each individual family develops its own sets of coping skills: from the ones used on big issues like how to balance freedom and structure, to the only slightly smaller ones like how and where to celebrate holidays, what to serve at meals, where to go on vacation, and how to plan and execute birthday parties, weddings, and funerals. But, unlike the workplace where it is pretty much required that the experienced person pass along a set of procedures to a newcomer to the job, families seem to take it for granted that the generations pick up the procedures, "the technology," by osmosis. It's not really that easy or automatic. And besides, since the Parent most children live with is only one member of an original family that may have had many more members, the "osmosis" approach leaves them, at best, with a one-dimensional picture of how things were done in one of the multidimensional families from which they have descended.

That is where Aunts and "transfer of technology" come into the picture. An Aunt demonstrates that the tradition she shares with a Niece's or Nephew's Mother or Father is bigger and more varied and more open to interpretation than anyone would be able to guess if that tradition had been passed along by only one person.

The Tastes of Childhood

I know, for example, that I will taste the tastes of childhood when I sit at the Christmas dinner table at my Sister's home. Somehow she has managed to remember the secret and duplicate the exact sort of turkey stuffing that we had as children. And it's not simply a matter of following a recipe. It's nothing short of alchemy. And I can never do it! So, if the family were depending on me, it would be lost.

On the "score one for the Aunt" side of the ledger, I seem to have a facility for remembering and repeating the special expressions and turns of phrase that belong to my birth family's oral tradition. In fact, one Christmas, after everyone in the family had grown weary of hearing me say, "As my Mother/or Father/or Aunt Maggie used to say . . . " I decided to put all the (highly distinctive) expressions down in a small booklet and give one to each Nephew and Niece. So, now all the people for whom my Parents form only 50 percent of their immediate ancestry will know that the "family" way of encouraging someone to trust in help from on high is to say, "Remember, God tempers the wind to the shorn lamb." So, you see, "transfer of technology" has many faces (and voices).

Sometimes this business of remembering and passing along family customs can have a funny side. Like the time Niece Meagen called home to Illinois from Dublin where she spending Thanksgiving while doing a season as an intern at one of the city's great theaters. "I can't remember the recipe for 'our turkey stuffing,'" she said (apparently with a straight face). Never mind that this otherwise enormously talented woman has only a passing acquaintance with a kitchen and that she was never seen to participate in any part of the rituals surrounding the Thanksgiving meal before the clearing of the table and washing of the dishes. She had a certain historian's sense of the importance of re-creating familiar recipes and proudly wanted to share the goodies with her Irish hosts. Which suggests that Aunts should not be surprised if, at some point, Nieces and Nephews look to them to have remembered and be willing to pass along the ways of doing things that belong to an earlier, nuclear family.

If your Niece asks you, as my Niece Alice once did long years after her Mother's untimely death, to recall a recipe your Sister had especially favored, don't hesitate to confess, as I had to, that you'd be hard pressed to remember even one recipe, but would find it easy to remember any one of a dozen of her favorite poems and would even be able to see, quite exactly, the handwriting in which she copied the poems into her journal. Not all parts of the family's "technology" are practical. And since my Sister Mary was strictly an "eat to live" person, it's unlikely that she would have contributed much in the line of recipes to the family's "bank" of coping skills. Great dreams and the appreciation of language were her departments. And that's also part of what an Aunt preserves and then transfers to her Nephews and Nieces.

"Transfer" or Consequences

How serious is it if an Aunt fails to transfer her family's "technology"? Judge for yourself. Consider some of the things an Aunt may have to cope with if she doesn't do her bit to ensure that ways of speaking, doing, celebrating, and just generally coping are kept in the family. Ask yourself some of these questions:

- How do you feel about birthday parties with expensive food and no presents? Or, expensive presents and no food? Or no food *and* no presents?
- How do you feel about the beloved, traditional Thanksgiving tuna? Topped off with the sparkling, aromatic Jell-O mold?
- How do you feel about the charming custom of the Aunt hosting the wedding reception?

- Why in the world would you be offended if someone chose to wear brilliant red to a family funeral?
- What's the big deal about mounting Great Grandmother's lace wedding veil on a broad-brimmed green straw hat?
- Would it really be disrespectful to have a "roast" instead of a standard memorial service?
- Why would you ever want to keep a collection of vinyls (oh, all right, "records," if you insist on calling them that)?
- Why not get rid of all those 1950s horrors at a garage sale?
- But, why would I have kept those photos? I didn't recognize anyone in them.

History is a fragile thing. That's why museums have curators. And one of the reasons why families have Aunts.

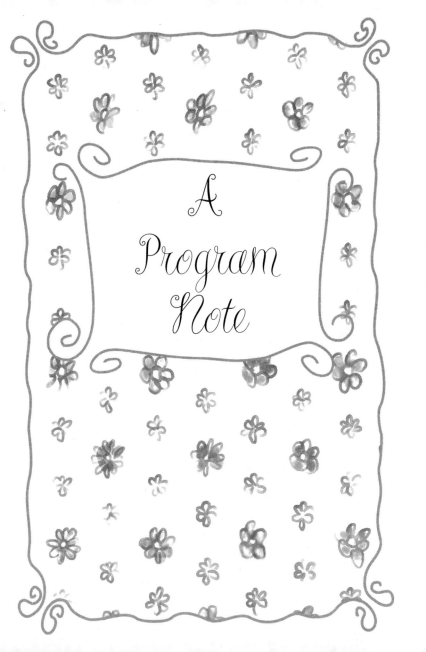

A

Program
Note

As in Dawn
(Versus Dusk)
A Pronouncing Guide
Part III

Since you're reading this chapter, it probably means you still haven't found the pronunciation for *Aunt* that matches your own. Or you may be in the market for a redo of the title you are currently using. If you redecorate your house, why not your familial titles? Which brings us to the "dawn" approach.

The Aunt as in Dawn (Versus Dusk) Option

For this pronunciation, the dictionary borrows *both* the *o* with a single dot above it (ȯ) *and* the *a* with two dots above it (ä), so you're really on your own with this one, but I think that . . .

In this case you call her (or are called) Aunt = Awnt.

This is the pronunciation Garrison Keillor uses when telling stories about Lake Wobegon on *A Prairie Home Com-*

panion. He manages to carry it off, but for most people, this version, Aunt = Awnt, is only workable as a stand-alone noun, not as a title used with a proper name. My feeling is that it was designed to refer to the *condition* of Aunthood and not any individual Aunt. I have heard people say, "As my Awnt always told me . . ." I've never heard it used conversationally as in, "Hurry up, Awnt Harriet; the train is pulling out." It's cumbersome.

If you are a person who likes to wear spats or hats designed for the Ascot races . . . to the movie theater in the mall . . . then, by all means, Aunt = Awnt could be just your cup of tea.

Consequences

If your name—or your Mother's or Father's Sister's name—is Dawn, don't even consider this one. Imagine the challenge of ever speaking the words "Awnt Dawn." It only gets worse if you consider names like Vonda or Tawanda. And it's totally impossible to imagine an "Awnt Debbie Sue."

Try not to use this one in gatherings including non-English-speaking people. It will only confuse them and confirm all their worst fears about the frustrating unpredictability of English pronunciation.

Playing in the Sequel

The role of the Aunt gives a good name to sequels. In other cases, the performances get less impressive as they go on. Not so with the Aunt, as a quick review of family history will reveal. Those early actresses are such an inspiration that they move the performers who follow them to stretch to reinvent the role in each new generation. It seems that the Aunt is just one of those roles that, once a woman has played it or seen someone else's remarkable performance of it, she wants to go on playing whenever possible. There is, of course, the slight problem of what to call the actress performing in the first sequel. But you can take it for "Graunted" that a solution is at hand.

A "Graunt" Proposal

A Short Suggestion for Replacing a Long Title

*M*om is Mom, Dad is Dad—it's simple. Even Grandparents usually manage to come up with a one-word identifier. The maternal ones are Nana and Gramps; the paternal are Gamby and Nono . . . or whatever. But, right from the start, it's always twice as complicated for Aunt Susan. And when Susan's Niece gives birth, what happens to Susan then? Is she Great-Aunt Susan or Grandaunt Susan? (Both titles are 300 percent more complicated than most familial tags, and each conjures up images of centenarians long past noting by Willard Scott.)

What I propose is the simple addition of "Gr" to the original title when one becomes a Great-Aunt (which I did long before I had to wear reading glasses to decipher a menu). To the original generation of siblings' children, then, one would be Aunt Demi. And to their children, Graunt Demi. Now, isn't that much easier?

Of course, it doesn't address what the Aunt in question is supposed to call that second generation of relatives. Are they Nieces squared? Or Nephews to the second power? In the spirit of simplification, why not just add an "n"? If people can accept a llama's two consonants, then why not a *Nniece's* or a *Nnephew's*? It also provides the opportunity for *Nnieces* and *Nnephews* to take a small tuition loan from the female relative and then impress everyone by being able to say, "I've come here to Overachiever's Prep as a result of my Graunt."

"Auntcestors"

"Aunt Annette, it's Victoria. For my third-grade history project, I need to interview an ancestor. May I interview you?"

When I recovered from the initial shock and stopped mentally cataloging geriatric homes I should start evaluating, I said, "Why, of course, Honey," and set a date to go over twenty-one questions about our family history with my nine-year-old Great-Niece and godchild. As I told the story later to my adult Nephew, he exhibited his usual charm and wit and said, without missing a beat, "She didn't mean *ancestor*; she meant *Auntcestor*, a very different thing." There was a great deal of truth in what he said, of course. I know, because I had a very remarkable "Auntcestor." My Aunt Catherine Margaret "Maggie" Doherty was the kind of woman any aspiring *Auntcestor* could study and from whose book she could take a leaf.

She wasn't the only Aunt I had, but she was the one I knew best, in spite of the fact that she lived an ocean away in Northern Ireland and was as unwilling to board a plane and come here as I was, for a long time, unable to afford doing the same to get to her. The Aunts on my Father's side of the family lived much closer, but one died before I was born and the other when I was still a little girl. By the time I finally met Aunt Maggie, I was an adult and she was in the last ten years of her life. But I knew her legend all my life and she managed to live up to every bit of it. In her, it is possible to see all the qualities of any really great *Auntcestor*. Accidents of history and geography aside, she will probably remind Aunts, Nieces, and Nephews alike of a really great *Auntcestor* in their own lives.

A Link to a Heritage

Part of the definition of an *Auntcestor* is providing a link to her Nieces' and Nephews' heritage. My Aunt Maggie was the youngest of her family, as I was of mine, so together we spanned a long expanse of family history. But, although born as the seventh of seven children, there was nothing of the "spoiled, youngest child" in her. She was always taking, inheriting, or being given responsibility for something or someone. And once she took it on, I suspect that not even God Almighty would have gotten her to relinquish it until her job was done, to her satisfaction.

In relation to us, her Sister's children, the "job" was to give us a visible and unforgettable link to the Ireland of their roots and ours. Being in her Northern Ireland birthplace, County Tyrone, and in Carrickone, the home where Mother and her siblings were born, is linked forever in memory to being with Aunt Maggie. She made that connection to the land become real. She was not just *from* that place; she was *of* it. Seeing the evidence of her bond, we understood better why she had always smiled indulgently and basically ignored us when, from time to time, we suggested that she come to live in the United States. And we understood that other part of ourselves that is not fully defined by the life we have lived here. The Aunt who remained in a Parent's native land is a special treasure for so many first-generation Americans. She exemplifies the fact that what your Parent came *from* is every bit as vital a part of your tradition as what he or she came *to*.

A Buffer Against Mortality

Aunt Maggie was, for her Sister's children, the reality of an older generation and, so, the buffer between ourselves and eternity. After our Mother had died, we could continue to hear the tone and cadences of her speech in this, her youngest Sister. At the same time, we could know the strength of this woman who had given up her nursing career in Belfast to take care of first one and then the next and the next of the people at that specific time and place who needed her. And lest you think there was a gram of saccharin in Aunt Maggie, she was the one who silenced the neighbors who asked her, when she had returned from the city to her tiny home community, about her plans to marry. She didn't spell out for them the remarkably small size or the uninspiring quality of the talent pool from which she was supposedly to select a life partner. She simply said, "I've given the matter a great deal of thought, and I have concluded that a clean want is better than a dirty breakfast." "Sweet," in other words, is not the word for Aunt Maggie. "Splendid" is. As it may very likely be for the *Auntcestor* who lives in your memory and comes to mind as you read these words.

A Standard of Measure

It's not an absolute requirement for aspiring *Auntcestors* that they give a luncheon after their own funerals. But, it surely feeds the legend as well as the mourners. Aunt Maggie could have been the poster person for independence. In life. And afterward. She lived from the land. Managed the people who worked it, when it was not so easy for a single woman to do so. Handed the Niece she had met just three years before a bank book and instructions on how to go to the bank manager and claim the cash that had been accruing from the modest income that came to her after she had sold the land (by private contract to a family she admired, mind you, not just to the highest bidder). And to round out the portrait, she left an envelope of cash with her friend Noreen Maxwell for a luncheon to follow her funeral. And if these stories seem focused on cash, let me remind you that in her case, cash was merely a symbol. A pallid reflection of the very vivid spirit of a brave lady. Which is why she has been cast in these pages in the role of the brave *Auntcestor* who will remind each individual of another, specific woman who would be "perfect for the part."

Because of the Aunt Maggies of life and the women like her, Nieces and Nephews have a claim to an inheritance their Parents alone could never give them. To aspiring *Auntces-*

tors, the Aunt Maggie "character" provides a road map for them to follow on the journey to being really great Aunts. An *Auntcestor* to link Nieces and Nephews to their past and give them courage to go toward their futures. Catherine Margaret "Aunt Maggie" Doherty was not the only Aunt I had. But she was surely the most inspiring.

A

Program
Note

As in Pest (at a Picnic)

A Pronouncing Guide Part IV

_S_till reading? That means you have studied and presumably rejected: Aunt = Ȯnt; Aunt = Änt; and Aunt = Awnt. All is not lost. There is still one option left. In fact, it may be the one that is top of mind for a great part of the country's population. Welcome to . . .

. . . The Aunt as in Pest (at a Picnic) Option

This is the first pronunciation the dictionary lists after the word. It's shown as an _a_ with no markings at all. It is the _a_ as in "Batman" or "Will you marry me?" or "sandbag."

In this case you call her (or are called) Aunt = Ant.

To be successful with this pronunciation, it helps to have been born in Illinois. And to have descended from three previous generations who were born there too. As someone raised by a first-generation American and a person who grew to young adulthood in Northern Ireland, I confess to revealing a *Janey-come-lately's* illness at ease with this pronunciation. I don't exactly get itchy from "Aunts = Ants," but I do get nonclinically schizophrenic. (That is, I recognize that it's what people expect to hear, but I don't feel entirely comfortable saying it.) In that, I suspect I'm not alone. While a goodly number of people use this version of the title, it probably sounds, even as they are saying it, a little more folksy and "down home" than they know themselves to be.

Judy Garland's references to "Auntie Em" are the most charming versions of this pronunciation. But, beware. The more adenoidal it sounds, and the closer that Aunt = Ant comes to being spoken as two syllables, the more certain it is to conjure up images of those highly socialized insects that live in colonies and love to come to picnics.

Consequences

If your given name also begins with an unadorned *A*, the one your speech teacher describes as "flat *a*,"— Aunt Ann, for example, or Aunt Annette—then this version of the title and your name, spoken together, sound about as attractive as the glamorous and haunting phrase "Cabbage Patch."

The affectionate form of the title, "Auntie," does not adapt well to this pronunciation. It sounds less like a title and more like a description of being in opposition, as in Auntie-Antiwar.

If you should ever decide to write a book about Aunts and mention that fact to strangers, using this version of the title, don't be surprised if they look at you quizzically.

They're wondering why you didn't choose a more winning subject . . . like ladybugs.

Finally, if you use this pronunciation, you leave yourself open to hearing, yet again, that most ancient, if not amusing, pun, "Speaking of insects, how is your Aunt?" I rest my case. But, after all, it's your call.

Reading the Reviews

Actors say they never read their reviews. Right. It's understandable, though. What are they supposed to say?—"Of course I read that review, and I thought it was egotistical, self-indulgent, and generally an exercise in the critic's liking to see his/her own pet phrases in print/hear the sound of his/her own voice." Nor is it likely that an actor will go public with the opinion that the "word of mouth" is so good that it should make people ignore the critics. Not so with at least one performer currently playing the Aunt. "If the word of mouth on Aunts is so good," she asks, "then why not honor them at least as heartily as we honor aardvarks?" As it turns out, it would take only a presidential proclamation to supply a permanent rave review.

Why Aardvarks but Not Aunts?

As recently as 1996, even aardvarks were doing better than Aunts.

I know, because in the directory of national anniversaries, dates, and observances, it was noted that March 3 was the start of "National Aardvark Week." This was not good news. Don't misunderstand: I wish nothing but the best to these distinctive living creatures. No one who has ever wished his or her nose to have a different appearance could be anything but sympathetic to an ant-eater. Nor was my reaction evidence of a deep-seated, Freudian resentment of them because of their name. Thus, it was unlikely to have been negative feedback from the country's Aunts that accounted for the absence of Aardvark Week in the 1997 edition of the directory.

Aardvarks were really just a symbol. It might as well have been elephants, who, the 1997 directory tells us, are honored on September 22—Elephant Appreciation Day. Of course, there's no reason to fail to pay tribute to these memorable pachyderms. They have been entertaining most of us since we attended our first circus. (And if you don't already have enough reasons to avoid picking on these mostly gentle giants, just catch a movie called *Elephant Walk* some evening on AMC and you will resolve never to cross one of these ivory-bearing mammals.) No, it's just that I can't help but believe that as a species, Aunts are at least as deserving of a day of honor as aardvarks or elephants.

But, wait; it gets worse. Just consider this list of a single year's specially designated "days" and see if you don't agree that honoring Aunts is at least an equal, if not a superior, reason for a national (or international, for that matter) observance.

January 22	**National School Nurse Day** To honor these keepers of the academic health.
February 12	**Nothing Day** To help people, currently known for nothing in particular, find imaginative ways to fill in the blanks in job applications.
March 22	**International Goof-Off Day** To mark a day for the encouragement of good-natured silliness.
April 15	**Rubber Eraser Day** To encourage people to use this invention by English chemist Joseph Priestley

to rub out a mistake on the income tax
form before mailing it today.

May 14   **National Receptionist Day**
To establish a celebration honoring the
frontline personnel of American business.

June 18   **National Splurge Day**
To encourage people to do something
indulgent.

July 24   **Cousins Day**
To honor all cousins, living and dead.

August 9   **Book Lovers Day**
To encourage people to borrow a book
or buy one and start reading it . . . or give
one as a gift.

September 22   **Proposal Day**
To honor unmarried adults everywhere
and to encourage men and women to propose marriage to their true loves on this
day.
    And in case you forget . . . the same
date is marked as *Elephant Appreciation Day*

October 16   **Dictionary Day**
To encourage people to own and use at
least one dictionary

November 7   **National Notary Public Day**
To recognize the fundamental contribution of notaries to the law and the people of the United States.

December 31   **Make Up Your Mind Day**
                  To encourage people who have a hard
                  time making up their minds to make one
                  decision and stick with it.

Obviously, some of the "days" designated for observances
have a vested interest at the heart of them. I can't help but
suspect, for example, that the "Sorry Charlie Day," observed
in honor of all people who have ever suffered rejection, just
might have something to do with the imaginative folks at
StarKist, home of Charlie's brand. But, really, aren't there
at least some equally enterprising people with a vested interest in honoring Aunts?

The way to get a really well-noted, recurring day in your
honor is to have it declared by presidential proclamation.
That is how we get the "biggies" like Mother's Day (by
annual presidential proclamation), Father's Day (by presidential proclamation, since 1971), and National Grandparents Day (by presidential proclamation, since 1979). It's not
entirely clear that Children's Day is proclaimed presiden-
tially, but it seems to be well established.

Congress used to be in the proclamation business, but
they opted out as of January 1995. And the number of presidential proclamations has been going down as well. So, if
Aunts are to gain a status at least equal to the aardvark and
the elephant, there's not a moment to waste.

Maybe it's time for AUNT-PAC, a political action com-
mittee designed to lobby for redress of the neglect of the
person who is, arguably, every family's best supporting
player. Perhaps Janet Reno or another Aunt who knows her
way around Washington, D.C., could be enlisted to head
AUNT-PAC.

Come to think of it, many a president would probably feel a certain affinity for a day honoring the Aunt. Among a virtual rogues' gallery of presidential relatives who told "all" or otherwise turned out to be a family embarrassment, I can't recall the name of a single presidential Aunt who did so. As noted earlier, Aunts have this amazing capacity to match the power of their "forgetories" to that of their memories. That talent alone would be reason enough to give them their own "day."

Think of it: the observance of "Aunt's Day" could include daylong recitals by Aunts of all and only the good qualities and the positive memories of their Nieces and Nephews. (I can feel the vast army of Nieces and Nephews out there warming to the idea already.)

Among the many things that became clear in the writing of this book is the fact that if Aunts were a film, there would have to be two- and three-page ads for it to accommodate all the rave reviews from critics. (How about "86 million thumbs up," for example?) The very mention of the word *Aunt* brings smiles to so many faces, loving stories to so many lips, and happy memories to so many minds. The sorority of Aunts is surely one of the proudest to which a woman can belong.

So . . . why not her own "day"?

Mr. President?

Hallmark?

Are you listening?

The Curtain Speech

*B*arbara Walters knows. She understands that listening to actors talk about how they got, learned, rehearsed, and performed their parts is roughly equal in fascination to watching the proverbial grass grow. Why else would she ask our favorite stars those potentially deadly questions about trees and legal cases and their preperforming lives?

Why, then, do you now find yourself at the end of a book that sets out to explore the role of *the Aunt*, from the point of view of one who is currently playing that role? Being a realist, I will put aside the possibility that you were riveted by the freshness of the insights and the stylishness of the prose. I believe that you are here, making a curtain call possible, because of the Aunts in your lives: the one you are, the ones you have, the ones you know; the ones of present, past, and future. They are a truly remarkable group of women. They have been there for you on a hundred yesterdays; are there for you now; and will, you trust, be there for you in the days to come.

Maybe the thing that ruined Cain (of Cain and Abel) was that he had no Aunt. Couldn't possibly have had one. But, that, of course, leaves us wondering how Abel survived the lack without resorting to murder. The fact is that the rest of us do have Aunts, real or honorary, who provide us with a unique connection to the world, who give us reasons to believe in the future of unconditional love and acceptance. At their best, they remind us that there are people out there who are particularly good at rejoicing in other people's good fortune.

And what of you who are Aunts yourselves? I believe that you are here for the curtain speech because you, above all, understand that the very definition of the role of *the Aunt* is as an ensemble player. You have personal knowledge of the fact that Aunting is never a solo endeavor. It comes about because of other people: their relationship to you by blood or by friendship, or both. It lives and flourishes because of other people: the Nieces and Nephews who came to you as gifts and continue to be gifts as they grow to become friends. You are here to honor the Aunts who moved you to become the Aunts you are. You are here because you hope to help your Nieces/Nephews become the people they can be. You are here because the book is just a beginning for you. You are the sequel. You are the movie. You are the living embodiment of what words can only approximate.

So, thank you all for being here. Each for his or her own reason. As an Aunt, I especially value what is done freely, by choice and with a smile. Now I would like to introduce my fellow players: my Parents, who gave me life, faith, hope, and love as well as Aunts; my Sisters, who gave me inspiration, Nieces, and Nephews; my Brother and guide, who gave me confidence that my words could communicate. I would like publicly to thank Peggy Fay and Meagen Fay for being my audience at rehearsals (and my critics and advisers). I would like to thank Kelly Freehill and Kara Leverte, who opened the doors; my editor, Aunt Sue Schwartz, who believed from the start, and Tante Maia Gregory, who made a gift of her wisdom and experience. I would especially like to thank God, Who gave me the cloud of a challenging year so that I could find in it the silver lining of time to write.